The NCEA *Catholic Educational Leadership* Monograph Series

The Vocation of the Catholic Educator

Richard M. Jacobs, O.S.A.

National Catholic Educational Association

Published in the United States of America by

The National Catholic Educational Association
1077 30th Street, NW, Suite 100
Washington, DC 20007
Copyright 1996
ISBN 1-55833-174-3

Richard M. Jacobs, O.S.A., Editor
Frank X. Savage, Series Supervisor

Production by Phyllis Kokus
Cover design by Beatriz Ruiz

Table of Contents

NCEA *Catholic Educational Leadership* Monograph Series: The Vocation of the Catholic Educator

Editor:

Richard M. Jacobs, O.S.A.
Villanova University

Series Supervisor:

Frank X. Savage
National Catholic Educational Association

Board of Advisors:

William Campbell, SM
Cupertino CA

Duane Schafer
Spokane WA

Joanne Cozzi, DC
Biloxi MS

Daniel Sherman
Seattle WA

Rosemary Donahue, SND
Portland ME

Sr. Joseph Spring, SCC
Mendham NJ

Lorraine Hurley
Naugatuck CT

Patricia James Sweeney, SSJ
Holyoke MA

Carol Kulpa
Memphis TN

Donald Urbancic
Towson MD

Helen Petropoulos
Ste. Genevieve du Bois
St. Louis MO

Mary Leanne Welch, PBVM
Dubuque IA

Editorial Assistant:

Mark Cataldi
Villanova University

Overview

The NCEA Catholic Educational Leadership Monograph Series: Reflective Guides for Catholic Educational Leaders

• the principal's importance...

Research studying the principalship reveals just how important principals are in fostering school improvement (Griffiths, 1988; Murphy, 1993: Smylie, 1992). Although the place where much of the action in schools transpires is in its classrooms (and hence, educational reformers focus largely upon what transpires in the teaching/learning context), much of the school's success seems to hinge largely upon the principal's ability to make sense of things in such a way that teachers become more effective in accomplishing in their classrooms what they are there to accomplish (Ackerman, Donaldson, & van der Bogert, 1996).

Perhaps principals figure so prominently in efforts to improve schooling because role expectations and personalities interact in a very powerful way, as Getzels and Guba (1957) argued nearly four decades ago. Or perhaps this effect is due simply to the eminence of the principal's office, given its focal prominence not only from an architectural perspective but also from a psychological perspective. While researchers suggest that principals do influence and shape life within schools in ways that no other single role, personality, or office can (Beck & Murphy, 1992), researchers are not at all unanimous about the conditions that make this so, as Foster (1980a, 1980b) astutely observes.

Whatever the actual reason may be, principals do occupy an important role, one vesting them with authority to articulate the school's fundamental purpose to a variety of constituents. In Catholic schools, principals may articulate this purpose at the opening liturgy of the school year and at the back-to-school night, pronouncing for all to hear "who we are," "what we shall be about," and, "the way we do things around here." Principals also reiterate their school's fundamental purpose while admonishing students or offering professional advice and counsel to their teachers. In the midst of a tragedy (for example, the death of a teacher, of a student's parent or pet, or as sadly is becoming all too frequent today, the violent and senseless death of a youngster), it is the principal who is expected to utter words of consolation on behalf of the entire school community. In these and many other situations, the principal's words can give deeper meaning to actions and events in terms of the school's purpose.

When principals effectively marshal the resources of their role, personalities, and office in leading others to share the school's purpose, teachers and students, for example, can direct their efforts toward achieving the school's goals. It is this synergy of efforts, Vaill (1986) argues, that sets "high performing systems" apart from mediocre or even good organizations. "Purposing," as Vaill describes this synergy, is that stream of leadership activities which induce in the organization's membership clarity and consensus about the organization's fundamental beliefs, goals, and aspirations (p. 91).

Without doubt, there are many Catholic school principals who capably articulate their school's purpose. In addition, these principals deftly manage what it means to be a member of the school community. In sum, these principals make it possible for others to identify their self-interest with the school's purpose.

• a threat to the school's Catholic identity...

For well over a century, religious women and men and priests have engaged in *Catholic* educational purposing, making it possible for generations of teachers and students to contribute to and experience great satisfaction and outstanding achievement as they have directed their efforts to fulfilling their school's Catholic purpose. For many teachers and students, the devotion of the religious sisters and brothers and priests inspired them to such an extent that the Catholic school's identity became identified with the selfless devotion of these men and women. And, rightly so.

However, in the decades following the close of the Second Vatican Council, the number of religious sisters and brothers and priests steadily declined. Meanwhile, the percentage of lay men and women who have committed themselves to the Church's educational apostolate increased markedly, although the total pool of Catholic schools (and hence, of teachers and principals) declined overall. While these trends indicate that some laity are generously responding to God's call to serve as educators in Catholic schools, as with all changes, new threats and opportunities emerge.

The exodus of religious sisters and brothers and priests from Catholic schools, however, is not the most significant issue that must be reckoned with. The paramount issue posed by this exodus concerns how the laity will receive the formation they need in order to preserve and advance the identity of the Catholic school. If lay principals are to lead their school communities to engage in *Catholic* educational purposing, they will need the philosophical, theological, and historical training that was part-and-parcel of the formation program for religious sisters and brothers and priests whose communities staffed Catholic schools. The formation that young religious received in prior generations, for better or worse, provided an introduction to the purpose of Catholic education, one that was intended to guide their decision-making once they would begin teaching and administering in Catholic schools. Without such a formative program, it is difficult to envision how, even the with the best of intentions, lay principals will engage in authentic Catholic educational purposing and foster their school's Catholic identity.

How, then, will the laity receive the formative training they need to teach and administer effectively in Catholic schools? In fact, teacher and administrator training can be undertaken at any college or university that sponsors these programs. Typical training includes an array of courses, field experiences, and internships designed to influence how an educator will deal with the problems of practice. In most places, teacher training commences during the undergraduate years when students select education as their major. On the other hand, administrator training programs begin at the graduate level, and most programs presuppose that the aspiring administrator has attained a sufficient teaching experience to be able to develop a richer and more complex understanding about what school administration really entails. Overall, the intention behind all professional training, whether it be for teachers or administrators, is to ensure that graduates possess the fundamental skills and knowledge that will enable them to practice their craft competently.

Competence, however, is only a first step. There are other important matters that educators must address as part of their work in schools, not the least of which is the substantive purpose for which we educate youth.

Aware of this need, administrator preparation is changing (Murphy, 1992; Prestine & Thurston, 1994). Many programs now introduce students to the notion of educational "purposing," as Vaill (1986) describes it, seeking to foster in students a consciousness that the principal's purpose in schools embraces "focusing upon a core mission," "formulating a consensus," and "collaborating in a shared vision." But, it must be remembered, purposing is not cheerleading. Instead, purposing necessitates translating a vision about substantive purposes into concrete activities.

How will Catholic principals receive the training that will qualify them to translate the "grammar of Catholic schooling" (Jacobs, 1995) into actions that symbolize the abstract values embedded in the Catholic school's purpose?

• the principal and Catholic educational purposing...

To bring the moral and intellectual purpose of Catholic schools to fruition, Catholic schools need principals who can lead their faculty and students to embrace and to be animated by the Catholic vision of life. This requirement presupposes, however, that Catholic principals have received training in the philosophical and theological purposes at the heart of the Catholic educational apostolate.

Honed through centuries of the Church's experience, some of these philosophical and theological purposes challenge current practice, requiring educators to consider why they do what they do in their classrooms and schools. Other Catholic educational purposes flatly contradict current notions about teaching and administering schools. If Catholic educational leaders are to provide leadership in the Catholic schools entrusted to their ministry, they need to know and understand why and how Catholic educational philosophy and theology stand critical of some current educational trends while being supportive of others.

In addition to the theological and philosophical purposes at the heart of the Catholic educational apostolate, principals of Catholic schools also need to be conversant with Catholic educational history, particularly as this drama has been enacted in the United States. The U.S. Catholic community's epic struggle to provide for the moral and intellectual formation of its students offers Catholic principals today instructive lessons about the culture and identity of the Catholic school, its purpose and importance, as well as what educators in Catholic schools ought to be doing for students. Conversancy with the experience of the U.S. Catholic community in its attempt to educate youth will enable Catholic school principals to place the issues confronting them within a larger historical context, to see how many of the issues they confront today have been dealt with in previous generations, and to respond to these issues in concert with the lessons that can be learned from Catholic educational history.

Earlier this century, when religious sisters and brothers and priests predominated the landscape of Catholic schooling, parents could assume with relative certainty that the school's principal, at least, was familiar with Catholic educational theology, philosophy, and history. In most cases, principals were familiar with these matters and provided educational leadership steeped in Catholic educational principles. Most significantly, their training provided them a background in the purposes underlying Catholic education and, as a consequence, enabled them to speak authoritatively about the school, its programs, and its effects upon students. Ironically, it was during this era that, while most knew what the Catholic school stood *for*, few worried about how it was managed. In striking contrast, as the public today worries more and more about managing schools and links this concept to quality education, the focus upon educational purposes becomes less important and quality schooling erodes. The evidence is clear: when the principal and faculty communicate and enact a compelling vision of schooling that coincides with parental interests, students benefit from the school's program (Bryk, Lee, & Holland, 1993; Coleman, Hoffer, & Kilgore, 1982; Coleman & Hoffer, 1987).

The threat posed by the loss of the religious sisters and brothers and priests who staffed Catholic schools during previous generations is something that can be dealt with. To meet the challenge, those charged with educational leadership within the U.S. Catholic community must provide formative training for aspiring and practicing Catholic school principals. They must be prepared to communicate the nature and purpose of Catholic education and to lead others to reflect upon the fundamental purposes that give life to and guide the Catholic educational apostolate.

• the evolution of the NCEA's *Catholic Educational Leadership* Monograph Series...

The NCEA's *Catholic Educational Leadership* monograph series has evolved from an extended conversation about this issue. Not only are the number of religious sisters and brothers and priests in school declining, the number of religious vocations is also declining. Rather than bemoan this trend, the Catholic community must look forward and prepare for a future that will be characterized by increased lay responsibility for many of the Church's temporal activities. Without doubt, if Catholic schools are to survive, the laity will have to respond to God's call and bear the responsibility for providing for the moral and intellectual formation of youth. In order to fulfill their call and its concomitant responsibilities, these men and women will need specialized formation to build upon the legacy bequeathed by their forebears.

Nationally, there have been many efforts to provide this type of formative training. The United States Catholic Conference has published a three-volume preparation program for future and neophyte principals, *Formation and Development for Catholic School Leaders*. Villanova University has sponsored the national satellite teleconference series, *Renewing the Heritage*, which brought together aspiring and practicing Catholic educational leaders with recognized experts from Catholic higher education. Several Catholic colleges and universities have programs specially designed to train Catholic educational leaders. The University of San Francisco's *Institute for Catholic Educational Leadership* stands as a prominent example of how Catholic higher education has worked to provide aspiring Catholic educational leaders the formation they need to lead Catholic schools. And, at the University of Notre Dame, the *Alliance for Catholic Education* has prepared young Catholic adults to teach in dioceses lacking Catholic educators. Maybe, in the long run, the *Alliance* will provide a new stream of vocations to the Catholic educational apostolate and perhaps some *Alliance* graduates will become the next generation's Catholic educational leaders.

But, for the present, the challenge remains: those who are called to serve as Catholic school principals deserve as much formative training as it is possible to provide them without duplicating already existing institutional efforts and depleting limited resources even further.

• who these monographs are intended for...

The NCEA's *Catholic Educational Leadership* monograph series is designed to supplement and extend currently existing efforts by providing access to literature integrating Catholic educational philosophy, theology, and history with the best available educational leadership theory and practice. Intended primarily for aspiring and practicing principals, the monograph series is also directed at other Catholic educational leaders: graduate students in Catholic educational leadership programs; superintendents; pastors; and, Catholic educators, parents, as well as members of Catholic school boards.

For principals, the monographs provide insight into the nature of educational purposing, albeit from a distinctively *Catholic* perspective. The variety of topics covered in the monograph series will present a wide breadth of ideas and practices conveying how principals might lead their schools to enhance their Catholic identity.

For graduate students in Catholic educational leadership programs and aspiring principals in diocesan-sponsored training programs, the monographs provide a compendium of philosophical, theological, and historical research describing the nature of educational leadership, again from a distinctively Catholic perspective. The bibliography provided in each monograph identifies where graduate students and participants in diocesan-sponsored training programs may find primary sources in order that they may put this valuable literature to practical use.

If the Catholic community is to provide formative training for educators in its schools, it is most likely that success will hinge largely upon the efforts of diocesan superintendents. As the chief educational officer of a diocese, each superintendent bears responsibility not only for the professional development of teachers and administrators who staff diocesan schools, but the superintendent also bears responsibility for their formative development as Catholic educators. Diocesan superintendents will find in the *Catholic Educational Leadership* monograph series an expansive array of ideas and topics that will not only challenge them to reflect upon how they exercise their leadership role but also how they might exercise that role by providing formative training for educators in diocesan schools.

Some pastors, particularly those who were ordained after the close of the Second Vatican Council, have not been exposed to Catholic educational thought and may feel uncomfortable, if not reluctant, to approach their congregations about educational issues. It must be asked: What could be of more importance to a pastor than the future of his congregation, that is, the children and young men and women who will grow into Catholic adulthood at the turn of the new millennium? In these monographs, pastors will discover provocative ideas intended to foster reflection upon how they might fulfill their pastoral responsibility to preach to their congregations about significant educational matters, whether or not their parish sponsors a Catholic school.

Finally, the NCEA's *Catholic Educational Leadership* monograph series endeavors to provide Catholic educators, parents, and members of Catholic school boards topical guides to stimulate reflection upon and discussion about the important educational responsibilities they bear. After having studied the materials contained in these monographs, it is hoped that these individuals will be enabled to make better informed decisions about what they ought to do on behalf of the young men and women God has entrusted to them. All too often, these important parental, Church, and civic responsibilities are relegated to public officials and faceless bureaucrats who have little or no acquaintance with or interest in enacting Catholic educational thought for the benefit of youth.

• inter-institutional collaboration on behalf of Catholic education...

Through the collaborative efforts of the Department of Education and Human Services at Villanova University and the NCEA's Chief Administrators of Catholic Education Department (CACE), outstanding Catholic educational theorists have been joined together in a long range project to provide Catholic educational leaders literature to spur their formation.

As series editor, Fr. Richard Jacobs, O.S.A., of Villanova University, has recruited outstanding Catholic educators to develop reflective guides that will enable principals to learn and to think about their important role in fostering school improvement, with a particular focus on their school's Catholic identity. His experience both as a teacher and administrator in Catholic middle and secondary schools as well as his work in Catholic higher education and as a consultant to Catholic dioceses and schools nationwide, have provided Fr. Jacobs the background to understand the formative needs of Catholic educational leaders and to translate those needs into successful programs. As the guest editor of the *Journal of Management Systems*, Fr. Jacobs has also amassed broad experience in shepherding texts from inception through publication.

Frank X. Savage, CACE Executive Director, is responsible for series supervision. In this role, Mr. Savage works with Fr. Jacobs to oversee the development of each monograph, ensuring that each monograph is not only theoretically beneficial but also of practical significance for aspiring and practicing Catholic educational leaders. His experience as an Archdiocese Secretary for Education as well as his work with Catholic superintendents nationally provide Mr. Savage the local and national perspective to oversee the development of a monograph series that will not duplicate but will enhance the projects and programs already functioning to form a new generation of Catholic educational leaders.

Assisting Fr. Jacobs and Mr. Savage are NCEA representatives experienced in Catholic school leadership. These individuals have been selected to review each manuscript once it has been developed. The critical feedback offered by the NCEA representatives helps Fr. Jacobs and Mr. Savage to work with the authors in order to ensure that the interests of each target audience will be met.

This inter-institutional collaborative effort on behalf of Catholic education is an important step forward. Bringing together representatives from Catholic higher education, a national Catholic educational organization, and seasoned Catholic educational leaders to develop a monograph series for aspiring and practicing Catholic educational leaders portends a good future. By sharing their different gifts on behalf of Catholic education, the Body of Christ will be enriched as Catholic educational thought is renewed in the formation of the next generation of Catholic educational leaders.

• using the monographs...

The volumes included in the NCEA's *Catholic Educational Leadership* monograph series are not intended to be scholarly reflections about the nature and purpose of Catholic educational leadership. While the monographs will include some scholarly reflections, they will also provide aspiring and practicing Catholic school principals practical guidance about how they might lead the men and women in their schools to engage in Catholic educational purposing.

Each monograph is written in a style that includes practical applications within the text. Each monograph is also formatted to provide reflective questions and activities along the expanded outside margins. These questions and activities have been included to help readers focus, in very practical ways, upon the important ideas and concepts being discussed. Readers are urged to take notes and to write down their thoughts and ideas as they read each monograph. Then, readers can return to their jottings and use them as they think about and plan to exercise Catholic educational leadership in the schools entrusted to them.

Were readers to complete and reflect upon the questions and activities included in the margins and to engage in the practical activities included in these monographs, readers of the NCEA's *Catholic Educational Leadership* monograph series would be better prepared to engage in Catholic educational purposing. They will not only have a more comprehensive understanding about the nature of Catholic educational leadership. They would also possess action plans for translating Catholic philosophical, theological, and historical ideals into actual practice in their schools. The ideals in each monograph, then, are not dogmatic pronouncements mandating what Catholic educational leaders are supposed to do. Rather, these philosophical, theological, and historical ideals are intended to stimulate reflective thought about what Catholic educational leadership involves and the principles upon which Catholic educational leadership might be exercised.

While the decline of religious sisters and brothers and priests in schools can be viewed as a threat to the future of Catholic education, the interest expressed by many lay men and women to follow in the footsteps of their forebears presents a tremendous resource and opportunity for the Catholic community. As the identity of the Catholic school is equated more with educational purposing than the fact of whether or not school's principal and teachers are religious sisters and brothers or priests, Catholic educational leaders can take advantage of the opportunity to form the new generation of Catholic educational leaders. These devoted men and women will carry forward the purpose of Catholic education into the 21st century, just as their forebears did at the turn of the 20th century.

On the Feast of St. Blase
February 3, 1996

Richard M. Jacobs, O.S.A.
Villanova University

Frank X. Savage
National Catholic
Educational Association

Providing for a Pressing Need: Theological and Spiritual Training for Catholic Educational Leaders

Today, the most pressing problem Catholic schools present to the average bishop is finances. It concerns him because funding Catholic schools is a concern for his pastors, one that consumes so much of their time and energy.

Even though financing Catholic schools is the principal problem today, an even more crucial problem looms on the horizon. To put this problem succinctly, we need to ask: How are we going to provide for the professional education and formation of the superintendents, principals, and teachers who will lead and staff our Catholic schools?

The professional preparation of teachers does not pose too much of a problem in this regard. Across the nation, almost every teacher in a Catholic school is fully certified. The professional preparation of Catholic school administrators and superintendents does present a problem, however. Their preparation requires a significant outlay of funds that can be hard to find in the pay envelope of the average Catholic school teacher or principal. But, if the funds are made available, then the academic program for their professional preparation is usually easy to find in most sections of the country.

Financing Catholic schools and the professional preparation of Catholic educators are problems that we can deal with, for the most part. The truly challenging problem involves how we will provide the theological and spiritual formation that is absolutely essential for future Catholic school leaders, if our schools are to be truly *Catholic* schools.

For years, the religious communities of women and men provided a solid grounding in faith and spirituality to those who would be entrusted with teaching and administering in Catholic schools. That rich religious formation continues to exert a tremendous effect in our schools. It is brought to bear not only by the women and men religious and priests who continue to serve in our schools, but also by the lay persons who were educated by them and who serve alongside them.

That tradition of solid Catholic spirituality, however, cannot be carried on by osmosis. As a Church and as an educational institution, we have to attend in a very intentional manner to the theological and spiritual formation of those who currently are or will be leading our schools in the very near future.

This need became particularly clear to me when I was working with some Catholic school teachers and administrators. We were involved in writing a defense or explanation of Catholic schools. During our discussions, it became obvious to me that at least a few of them were not familiar with the basic philosophy of Catholic education. They were delighted, however, to discover that there was available a long tradition of thinking about Catholic education.

They would be even more delighted to find in one place—between the covers of this monograph—an inspirational summary of Catholic thinking about the vocation of the Catholic educator. And once teachers and administrators appreciate what their vocation means, they will have no difficulty in articulating a rationale for Catholic schools.

This monograph, *The Vocation of the Catholic Educator*, is not intended as an apologetic tool. It is meant to help Catholic educators move from competence to excellence. This move occurs when the educator is able to "define, strengthen, and articulate those enduring values, beliefs, and cultural strands that give the school its unique identity over time" (Sergiovanni, 1995, p. 88).

By now, many neutral observers agree that there is something about Catholic schools that makes them better than it might be predicted, though there is less agreement about what that something is. Perhaps it is precisely the Catholic culture with its values and beliefs that endow each educator with a mission and challenge each of them to view every student as destined for eternal life in God. Without doubt, a student has to be challenged by and to feel a special sense of belonging in that kind of school community. So, too, must teachers and administrators.

The author of this monograph, Father Richard Jacobs, O.S.A., not only lays out those values and beliefs that give Catholic schools their culture and identity; he also describes practical ways for Catholic educators to make this culture and identity their own. The key, he argues, is a daily mindfulness about the spiritual mission of the Catholic school, a mission rooted in the basic Christian virtues of faith, hope, and charity.

The courts of our country and the opponents of any public financial assistance to parents who choose a Catholic school for their children often characterize what happens in our schools as "indoctrination" and describe it as "pervasive." In the penultimate section of this monograph, Fr. Jacobs recommends that something be pervasive in our schools, that is, a spirit of personal caring that invites students to enter into a fuller, richer, and more hope-filled understanding of life.

The Vocation of the Catholic Educator should be in the hands of every principal and maybe every teacher in our schools. The scriptural reflections on the vocation of the Catholic educator are reason enough to recommend it. Most importantly, this monograph is a cogent reminder that for those who teach and administer in Catholic schools, the secret of educational excellence is discipleship.

I am deeply grateful to the National Catholic Educational Association for sponsoring the *Catholic Educational Leadership* monograph series of which this is the first volume. The series addresses a most pressing need. If the monographs that will be included in this series are as solid and helpful as this inaugural volume is, the association will have made another outstanding contribution to Catholic education.

An eighth grade student in one of our diocesan schools wrote about Catholic education. Her essay proves that the message Catholic educational leaders proclaim does get through:

> Catholic schools are a lot more than just learning about God and our religion. It's about getting along with others and expanding our faith. Yes, we learn about math, reading and history, but also how to live more freely in a world of sin and hatred.
>
> Catholic schools are great in our society because they teach us kids how to be role models and teach us how to live the faith. We have to try to love in a world with peace, love, and forgiveness. We can't go out and hit or shoot someone just because of their race or culture.
>
> ...If we take this all in, it seems a little much, but for our Catholic schools, it's all in a days work.
>
> *-Sara Hendricks, St. Paul, Wrightstown, WI*

Sara's essay makes the financial struggles of parents, bishops, pastors, and parishioners to make a Catholic education available to youth a very worthwhile effort.

† Most Reverend Robert J. Banks
Diocese of Green Bay
Chair, USCC Committee on Education

Chapter 1

The Vocation of the Catholic Educator: The Heart of Excellence

Ask teachers and administrators about educating youth and they'll probably tell you that "it's no simple job." While many noneducators would like the public to believe that there is "one best way" to educate youth and all that we have to do is to impose it upon schools, authentic education requires very hard work. In particular, it requires educators who engage in deliberative decision-making, that is, selecting the best option from among many possible alternatives (Burlingame & Sergiovanni, 1993).

In many schools today, teacher and administrator decision-making has increasingly been routinized, stultifying what are perhaps the most creative and nurturing aspects of the educator's vocation. As a consequence, the ideals and values that once motivated teachers and administrators to devote their lives to the formation of youth have gradually grown tepid and sometimes cold. And, as teaching and administering in the nation's elementary and secondary schools have been gradually and oftentimes painfully reduced to functional, rote decision-making, the purpose for teaching and administering in schools has eroded. Almost imperceptibly,

- educating youth has become instructing them;
- "how we do things around here" has replaced serious reflection upon the school's purpose and adapting it to current realities;
- contracts and formal relationships have defined jobs and responsibilities; and,
- membership in the school feels more like belonging to a cold, impersonal, bureaucratic organization than it does living in a warm, personal, vibrant community.

Given this sterile climate, authentic deliberation about what ought to be done for youth has disintegrated. A predictable school routine now runs everything on automatic pilot. Passion for and conflict over fundamental purposes is absent from discussion. Is it any wonder, then, that students become disillusioned, bored, and achieve less in those schools where their teachers and administrators think more about getting through the day than doing what's best for their students today?

To the degree this caricature accurately portrays life in any school, educational decision-making lacks a transcendent purpose or value. No longer is it authentic, responding to real people with real difficulties, in real situations. Instead, educational decision-making is reduced to providing rote answers to generic people who have pre-determined problems, based upon statistical laws of averages. The substantive foundation at the heart of educating youth, its guiding ethic, has sadly become absent.

Over two decades ago Silberman (1970) noted this failure, candidly observing how educational practice had lost its touch with its substantive roots:

> If teachers made a botch of it, as an uncomfortably large number do, it is because it never simply occurs to more than a handful to ask *why* they are doing what they are doing, to think seriously or deeply about the purposes or consequences of education.
>
> This mindlessness—the failure to think seriously about educational purpose, the reluctance to question established practice—is not the monopoly of the public school; it is diffused remarkably through the entire educational system, and indeed the entire society.
>
> If mindlessness is the central problem, the solution must lie in infusing the various educating instructions with purpose, more important, with thought about purpose, and about the ways in which technique, content, and organization fulfill or alter purpose. (italics in text, p. 11)

As "mindlessness" is the exacerbating disease for Silberman, it may well be that "mindfulness" is its antidote. For teachers and administrators, mindfulness would mean breaking out of the straightjacket of mindlessness by standing for something—what Silberman has called "purpose"—and using this purpose to inform and guide their decision-making process.

In this monograph we will explore the vocation of the Catholic educator, examining what is the heart of the Catholic educational ministry as well as what it is that Catholic teachers and administrators should be mindful about. Throughout, we will assume that Catholic educators, especially those who serve in Catholic schools, are, for the most part, competent practitioners of the fundamental skills associated with good schooling (Bryk, Lee, & Holland, 1993; Coleman, Hoffer, & Kilgore, 1982; Coleman & Hoffer, 1987; Convey, 1992; Willms, 1984, 1985, 1987).

What we will not assume, however, is that Catholic educators are always as mindful about what their vocation requires as they are about what their work requires. For Catholic educators, mindfulness of their vocation, the purpose that motivates men and women to serve as teachers and administrators, is what will enable them to build upon their fundamental pedagogical and administrative competence and to lead their school communities to fulfill their substantive purposes. Hopefully, the ideas shared in this monograph will stimulate Catholic educators to become more mindful and deliberative about their vocation so that their daily activities will reflect ever more perfectly the substantive "*why*" that is the heart of the functional "*what*" they do for youth.

The rationale is simple: as Catholic educators become mindful of the divine call that is the heart of their professional practice, they will then be able to concretize in even more explicit ways the mission for which they have devoted their lives as ministers of the Gospel. Each day, they and their students will have a purpose for engaging in the activities that are part of their school's life.

Were this ideal to be realized in every Catholic educator's decision-making process, several indicators of educational excellence would be present. These include:

- rote decision-making would be superseded by deliberative inquiry into the educator's mission;
- "how we do things around here" would continuously evolve as teachers and administrators adapt what they do to fulfill the school's purpose as well as to meet their students' needs;
- an educational covenant would shape shared responsibilities within the school community; and,
- responsive leadership would characterize the decisions made by teachers and administrators.

These indicators of excellence are not happenstance outcomes dictated by the fates. Neither can these indicators simply be wished into existence. Excellence emerges as educators are mindful of their vocation and use this theological purpose to decide what they will do.

To foster mindfulness as well as to encourage reflective inquiry into the vocation of the Catholic educator, we will first examine the context within which schooling transpires. In particular, we will focus upon Sergiovanni's (1995) distinction between educational competence and excellence, developing a foundation for teachers and administrators to reflect upon the functional and substantive aspects of their work.

But, skills development and educational competence are not the focus of our endeavor. Instead, these notions are the point from which Catholic educators may reflect upon and evaluate their efforts as well as the degree to which they are truly fulfilling their school's substantive purpose. This reflective work provides the context from which Catholic educators can become more mindful of their vocation as well as how the substantive aspects of their practice build upon their fundamental competence and contribute to the attainment of educational excellence.

Our focus will then shift from this theoretical discussion about

---

Identifying a reflective context:
- *As an educator, what motivates you? What is your focus as a new school year begins?*
- *What would a "culture of excellence" look like in your classroom? in your school?*
- *Describe a situation where you became mindful that your vocation required more of you than simply providing instruction for youth.*
- *How do these ideals relate to your vocation as a Catholic educator?*

educational competence and excellence to a consideration of selected scriptural texts and Church documents. Familiarity with these documents provides Catholic educators the opportunity to reflect upon the substantive responsibilities they bear as *Catholic* educators. As they read these ideals, some teachers and administrators might think about how they could collaborate in using the ideas contained in these documents to engage their colleagues in communal reflection about their school's fundamental purposes. Were a school's entire staff to engage in this deliberative practice, they might themselves be in a better position to forge a more mindful and comprehensive understanding about the substantive purpose that is the heart of their ministry.

In the monograph's closing section, we will examine some practical activities that can help Catholic educators to focus upon their vocation as they learn to become more mindful of why they do what they do. The challenge seems so simple: by reflecting upon their vocation, teachers and administrators will become more mindful about the substantive dimensions of education that ought to be reflected in the functional activities they engage in day-in and day-out. At the same time, though, this challenge is also very idealistic: educators will become for their students today, as their forebears did in previous generations, authentic witnesses to the salvific effect that faith, hope, and love offer young men and women.

In contrast to those one-shot workshops and inservice activities that offer the false promise that they will "professionalize" education, the discipline of being mindful about one's vocation and striving to inculcate its demands into educational decision-making requires much more than an inspiring pep-talk or skills training session. Catholic educators will need time to engage in deliberative inquiry into the substance of their vocation. They will also need patience, in dealing with one another and their students, if their words and actions are to herald for youth the educator's purpose for being in the school in the first place. And, they will need to be persistent as other matters vie for their attention, attempting to distract them from focusing upon the substantive aspects of their work.

The vocation of the Catholic educator is the heart of educating youth. It is a call from God that challenges teachers and administrators to be for youth something that is both simple and idealistic, yet something both practical and full of hope. This is the heart of educational excellence. In the middle of this very difficult and challenging ministry, tangible rewards are meager. But, these disciples possess an educative vision illuminated by the theological virtues of faith, hope, and love. They know that, when the Lord comes to gather His people into the peace of God's kingdom, those who "have only done our duty" (Luke 17:9) will find the fulfillment of their deepest longings in the peace of God's kingdom. This is the eternal reward they truly seek.

Chapter 2

The Context: Competencies and Functional Behaviors...Excellence and Substantive Behaviors

Though teachers and administrators in schools serve in different roles and capacities, having different expectations, both are devoted to a common mission: educating youth. Competence in this common endeavor, whether as a teacher or as an administrator, cannot be overlooked. It is the solid foundation upon which educational excellence is built.

• for teachers...

When school commences late each summer, novice teachers set foot in their classrooms for the very first time. With their pre-service and student teaching experiences behind them, nearly all of these neophytes possess an ardent desire to devote their efforts to the task of becoming good teachers. Perhaps their pre-service experiences have enabled these neophytes to realize that they are undertaking a rather formidable endeavor. Hazy idealism, however, beclouds their vision early in their professional career only because they have not yet accumulated enough practical experience concerning what being a *good* teacher actually entails.

For the most part, the greater majority of novice teachers need to develop competence in at least three skills: classroom management, human relations, as well as the pedagogical skills associated with good curriculum and effective instruction. Throughout the course of their first five years on the job, neophyte teachers spend much of their time and energy focusing upon and developing competence in these important skills as they struggle through their successes and failures to become good teachers (Kagan, 1992).

Eventually though, most of these novice teachers survive their first few years. They become the dependable veteran faculty who return each fall to devote their talents to yet another year of providing for the intellectual and moral formation of youth. But, if these dependable veterans wish to become more than good teachers, that is, if they desire to become excellent teachers, they must be willing to undertake an even

> *Recall your first years as a teacher.*
> - *What issues were you most concerned about and became your primary focus?*
> - *Reflecting upon your early teaching experiences, how would you evaluate your performance?*
> - *What were your talents and strengths? What areas did you need to improve upon?*
> - *In view of this, what advice should your principal have given you?*

more daunting endeavor than that which confronted them during their first few years of teaching.

Veteran instructors, skilled as they are in managing their classrooms, relating well with their colleagues and a disparate group of students, and utilizing a diversity of pedagogical methods to provide instruction for their students, must also engage in continuous professional learning. Rather than merely perfecting these skills, veteran instructors must now become conscious about how their words and actions communicate symbolically their school's cultural purposes. Developing adeptness with the symbolic and cultural skills associated with educating youth (and building as these two skills do upon basic instructional competence) is what will transform these good teachers into excellent ones.

Excellent teachers, then, enter their classrooms year after year. They are recognized as specialists, having demonstrated their prowess in classroom management, human relations, and curriculum and instruction. But, more importantly, they also are very conscious of and sensitive to the significance of their role as mediators of the general culture. These are the educators who provide those moral and intellectual lessons that will influence their students' lives and shape their decisions as adult citizens.

It takes time to develop excellent teachers, those professional educators who understand and act in accord with the values and expectations that are incumbent in their symbolic and cultural roles. For these veterans, excellence demonstrates itself as they build upon their skilled competence and continuously struggle to convey authentic educational experiences that stimulate their students' learning.

It is the craft of designing authentic educational experiences which calls forth from an educator's soul the substantive aspects of the teacher's vocation. Becoming an excellent teacher is the culmination of a life's calling, one that manifests itself daily as these teachers provide authentic moral and intellectual lessons for their students.

• for administrators...

Like their colleagues whose primary responsibilities lie in their classrooms, good school administrators also begin each new school year possessing high expectations about what they and their colleagues might be able to accomplish during the course of the upcoming year. Perhaps they have devised plans to inaugurate a novel approach to supervising and evaluating faculty, to implement a new schedule, to improve the student advisement process, or even, to engage in curriculum development.

Even with well-crafted plans to build upon the previous year's achievements and to improve upon its shortcomings, school administra-

> *Recall your early experiences as an administrator.*
> - *What issues were you most concerned about and became your primary focus?*
> - *Reflecting upon your early administrative experiences, how would evaluate your performance?*
> - *What were your talents and strengths? What areas did you need to improve upon?*
> - *In view of this, what advice should your superintendent have given you?*

tors undertake each new year knowing that three important administrative competencies will be put to the test: school management skills, human relations skills, and instructional leadership skills. During the course of the academic year, the interaction of people and events will reveal whether school administrators possess competence in these skills and, thus, fulfill the role expectations and organizational responsibilities delegated to them.

Over the course of the years, competent administrators can devote their talents toward forming an authentic and deliberative community of educators, one dedicated to the moral and intellectual formation of youth. To achieve this important goal, however, if *good* administrators desire to become more than good at what they do, that is, to become *excellent* administrators, they must be willing to undertake an even more challenging endeavor than that which confronted them when they first accepted administrative responsibility for their schools. Like their colleagues in the classrooms, these administrators, too, must now become more conscious of and reflect through their words and actions the symbolic and cultural roles that will transform good school administration into administrative excellence.

Excellent administrators are present in schools not merely as specialists who have been skilled in school management, human relations, and instructional leadership. Moreover, excellent administrators are also consciously aware that they mediate, by their presence and deliberative acts within the school environment, something more important and necessary than simply a managerial presence. School administrators are not merely their school's supervisors, bearing responsibility for its smooth functioning. Through their symbolic role, excellent administrators also embody the values and engage in those behaviors that communicate the cultural purposes for which their schools were established. Through their cultural role, excellent administrators mediate, through their words and actions, the fundamental beliefs, assumptions, and values that distinguish their schools from other, even similar, schools. In short, excellent administrators infuse the values incumbent in their symbolic and cultural roles into what they do.

Administrative excellence, then, manifests itself in the way administrators relate with teachers, staff, students, parents, and the larger community as well. For example, these administrators genuinely care for others and express concern that all members of the school community care for one another. These administrators act and expect others to act in an honest, open, and collegial manner. They also struggle to include all members of the school community in its activities to the degree that is possible. Finally, excellent administrators are committed to inquiring about what is truly going on in their school in order that authentic learning might transpire within it (Sergiovanni, 1994, p. 71).

• a common mission...

As this theoretical distinction between competence and excellence has implied, when educators collaborate to express the fundamental beliefs, assumptions, and values distinguishing their educational community from others and communicate the basic purpose for which their school exists, all of the management skills, human relations skills, pedagogical skills, symbolic skills, and cultural skills coalesce as "forces" (Sergiovanni, 1995). Taken as a whole, these five forces have the net effect of inducing clarity, consensus, and commitment regarding the school's fundamental purpose (Vaill, 1986).

As this distinction relates to educators in general, excellence in teaching and administration is more than developing professional skills about what ought to be done in classrooms and schools or a template to be imposed upon them. In the real world of schools, excellence is something that is discovered as the educational community, whose members (including students, teachers, administrators, support staff, and parents), seek to understand *why* they do *what* they do and to make that substantive purpose the foundation for all of their educational decision-making.

But, for Catholic educators, men and women whose presence in classrooms and schools is predicated first upon a divine initiative, excellence requires more. As men and women of faith, hope, and love, they stand before one another as living symbols of what the Catholic faith assumes, believes, and values to be true. And, as a consequence of this shared vision, they form an educational community that devotes its efforts to the fulfillment of its theological purpose. That is, they strive to provide youth the moral and intellectual formation that will enable them one day to fulfill their vocation not only as citizens of a nation, but also citizens of God's kingdom. They know that their students today will be the next generation's disciples, continuing to proclaim the Good News which has been entrusted to them through the generous ministry of this generation's Catholic educators.

Chapter 3

Excellence Builds Upon Competence: A Theoretical Perspective

Sergiovanni (1995) uses Maslow's hierarchy of prepotent needs (1943) and Herzberg's two-factor theory of human motivation (1966) as his foundation for conceptualizing a distinction demarcating *good* educators from *excellent* ones. As this distinction was introduced in the preceding section, Sergiovanni's two-level, five-step model provides a vantage not only to look at what good educators seek to do, but also, to understand what it is that sets excellent educators apart from their colleagues. For our purposes here, Sergiovanni's distinction provides a theoretical context to appreciate not only what Catholic teachers and administrators do but, more importantly, why they are doing it. His distinction also makes it possible for us to conceptualize theoretically what educational excellence truly entails for Catholic educators.

First the model.

• the good educator...

Educational competence forms a base upon which educational excellence is crafted (Figure 1). This model's foundation consists of competencies related to three skills: management skills (e.g., planning, organizing, budgeting), human relations skills (e.g., dealing with conflict, providing feedback, maintaining positive regard, motivating), and technological skills (e.g., curriculum development, instructional methods). Each of these skills, in dynamic interaction with the others, manifests itself in the daily repertoire of "good" teachers and administrators. These three skills are the "forces" which ensure that the school and its classrooms operate effectively, that the members of the school community experience support, encouragement, and challenge, and that curriculum and instruction reflect expert professional knowledge (Sergiovanni, 1995, pp. 84-87). As educators demonstrate competence in each of these three sets of skills over a period of time, they become regarded as the truly *good* educators, which indeed they are.

Thus, good educators are focused intently upon *what* they do. They organize their school and its classrooms so that people, the teaching process, and the learning experiences function in a unified manner to promote student growth. Good educators also foster the kinds of

> *Reflect upon your school and its classrooms.*
> - *Is it managed well? Are there organizational problems that make it impossible to focus upon issues of substance?*
> - *Do the faculty, staff, students, and parents get along? Are there any human relations issues that make it difficult for the school's purpose to be reflected in people's relations with one another?*
> - *Are your school's curricular objectives being met? Are the classrooms characterized by wonder and excitement?*

Reflect upon your practice:
- *Do the forces of educational competence influence how you plan your daily repertoire?*
- *What area(s) do you experience yourself needing to develop?*
- *What elusive goals are you are pursuing?*

communication between and among themselves, as well as with their students, that develops into a form of communicative competence serving to promote their students' growth and development across a wide array of inter- and intra- personal domains. Finally, good educators know and understand that curriculum and instruction are a means to a desired end. And so, they carefully craft the learning environment, given the shifting tides of personalities, dispositions, and the diversity of attitudes present in their schools and classroom at any particular moment. Where educators demonstrate competence in each of these three critical skills, students, parents, and other interested parties easily recognize what these educators are able to accomplish.

At the same time, while others recognize and might even seek to reward good educators, these individuals never seem to be quite satisfied with the outcomes of all of their efforts. For example, even in the midst of their success, good educators relentlessly question whether they have managed their classrooms and schools well, met each student's unique needs, or conveyed their lessons as they had planned. Good administrators, too, are always on the hunt—looking for ways to improve things around the school without upsetting its smooth functioning. Thus, good educators seem to be striving for an elusive goal (i.e., educational excellence), one that always seems just beyond their grasp. But, it wasn't beyond the reach of those exemplars who inspired them to become educators!

Figure 1.

THE FORCES OF EDUCATIONAL COMPETENCE
"What educators in schools do well"

3. *Good Curriculum and Instruction*:
   Pedagogical skills are used to craft an interactive and stimulating learning environment for both students and teachers.
2. *Good Human Relations*:
   Administrators, teachers, students, and parents respect one another and communicate well with one another about important matters.
1. *Good School and Classroom Management*:
   Every structure is designed to serve the school's primary purpose: educating students. Evaluation concerns whether the structure serves this primary objective.

Adapted from: T. J. Sergiovanni. (1995). *The principalship: A reflective-practice perspective* (3rd ed.). Needham Heights, MA: Allyn and Bacon.

For good educators, change isn't all that dramatic or threatening, simply because it is a regular part of their routine. Taking heed of Senge's (1990) admonition that "slower is faster," their approach to change is transformational. They experiment and practice, achieving a continuous series of small wins that exert high leverage upon the status quo (Weick, 1984). They lead their colleagues by example, seeking to improve school functioning in substantive ways.

• the excellent educator...

For Sergiovanni (1995), excellence is built upon fundamental competence and begins to emerge as good educators become more consciously aware of their purpose for being in their classrooms and schools and strive to infuse this awareness into everything they do and say (Figure 2). Excellence, however, is not something created *ex nihilo*. Instead, it requires teachers and administrators who think about and struggle together to achieve their school's purpose as they engage in the hard work of educating youth.

Excellent teachers and administrators "want to know what is of value to the school...they desire a sense of order and direction, and they enjoy sharing this sense with others" (Sergiovanni, 1995, p. 87). They embody their symbolic roles by "selective attention or the modeling of important goals and behaviors, and signaling to others what is important and valuable in the school" (p. 87). Thus, in a school where there is an order exerting its influence, teachers and administrators use their symbolic role to enable other members of the school community to make sense out of what they are doing and to contribute their human resources to achieving the school's purpose.

The educator's cultural role, on the other hand, takes the symbolic role one step further. The cultural role involves how teachers and administrators "define, strengthen, and articulate those enduring values, beliefs, and cultural strands that give the school its unique identity over time" (Sergiovanni, 1995, p. 88). Teachers and administrators do this as they clarify and articulate their school's purpose, socialize new members, tell stories and develop myths about people and events that are embedded in the school's history, explain "the way things are around here," unveil symbols conveying the school's purpose and what it has meant to its members, and reward and punish members. With persistence, the "school and its purposes become revered, and in some respects they resemble an ideological system dedicated to a sacred mission" (p. 88).

Thus, as educators focus upon and clarify their school's purpose, behaviors, attitudes, and artifacts can be made to represent more explicitly the school's intangible purpose. For example, an intolerance for fighting, gossiping, and disrespect as well as the school's crest, its

In all of their activities, excellent educators stand for and symbolize the school's purpose.

- *Cite instances where you have experienced how your school is a place for learning, not only course related materials, but more importantly, how to live life according to true principles.*
- *Identify situations where you have found teachers and students being passionate about what their school means to them.*
- *What does your school's seal, trophies, and other artifacts as well as its architecture, stand for and suggest about the school's purpose?*
- *Are your school's policies, procedures, and handbooks consistent with the school's purpose statement? Are important classroom and administrative decisions clearly related to these documents?*

11

In everything they do, "excellent" educators communicate their purpose.
- *Are the matters discussed at administrative meetings focused upon issues directly related to the school's purpose? Or, do these meetings tend to become mired down in administrivia?*
- *Identify how administrators, teachers, students, and parents are made aware of and how they express the school's purpose in their words and actions.*
- *Describe how your school's purpose is expressed in each classroom's distinctive environment.*

architectural design, and its trophy cases can all serve as potent reminders of precisely what it is that the school stands for, positively as well as negatively. For excellent educators, their symbolic and cultural roles work in tandem to promote and enhance their school's purpose.

To grasp Sergiovanni's (1995) insight into how these two forces operate in classrooms and schools, let us consider how conversations between educators might make their school's symbolic and cultural forces more explicit.

It is not unusual for educators to complain to one another that they just don't understand why a particular student or grade level isn't paying attention. At other times, while one educator may be engaged in an animated tirade, complaining bitterly about why students are failing to take things seriously, another educator may be expressing outrage about student development, their extracurricular lives, and their interests, too. On other occasions, while a group of educators may verbally trace classroom problems to parental attitudes and dispositions, or even to the world at large, another educator may interrupt, making a definitive judgment about other colleagues, expressing frustration that their attitudes promote dissension in the school and should not be tolerated. At first blush, all of this banter may not appear terribly professional. In fact, were outsiders to overhear some of the typical banter that educators engage in with one another, whether it be in the faculty room, lunch table, corridor, or parking lot, they might be scandalized.

However, this banter is not necessarily pejorative, expressing an arrogant and condescending "we're always right, they're always wrong," "us-against-them" attitude. For if one listens carefully to what follows much of this banter, one might detect the forces of excellence that demarcate excellent educators from their otherwise disgruntled, blame-finding colleagues. Excellent educators, for example, offer one another solace, deliberate about possible resolutions, strategize about potential positive and negative outcomes, and challenge one another's viewpoints. Many times, excellent educators depart for their homes or classrooms understanding perhaps just a little bit better what they need to enact in their schools, classrooms, or in their relations with one another and their students, if they are to bring their school's purposes to bear through their teaching and administering.

Sergiovanni (1995) reminds us that what excellent teachers and administrators are struggling to achieve is to form the character of their students and colleagues. They realize that they stand before their students and one another as symbols of what the school community and the larger culture value. All of their storytelling, mythmaking, and psychoanalyzing has more to do with enacting a culture of educational excellence than it does formal education *per se*. Parents and students, who normally aren't privy to much of the typical banter that transpires between educators, notice the outcome. They recognize and comment that these educators "care about the students."

When educators have developed expertise in the symbolic and cultural skills that enable them to communicate with their students and colleagues what the school community assumes, believes, and values, these educators also convey the heritage of what it means to be a human being within that particular school community. "As persons become members of this strong and binding culture, they are provided with opportunities to enjoy a special sense of personal importance and significance. Their work and their lives take on a new importance, are characterized by richer meanings, an expanded sense of identity, and a feeling of belonging to something special" (Peters and Waterman cited in Sergiovanni, 1995, p. 89). It is through these and many other such behaviors, attitudes and artifacts that excellent educators manifest the substance of their vocation to educate youth.

Figure 2.

THE FORCES EVIDENT IN EXCELLENT SCHOOLS
"*Why* educators in excellent schools do what they do"

5. *A Medium of Culture*:
   The school and all the activities of its members stand for and represent cherished ideals.
4. *Symbols that Speak*:
   Tangible artifacts (e.g., school motto, insignia, crest, architecture, educators) convey the core assumptions, beliefs, and values guiding educational practice in the school.

Adapted from: T. J. Sergiovanni. (1995). *The principalship: A reflective-practice perspective* (3rd ed.). Needham Heights, MA: Allyn and Bacon.

In short, excellent educators are mindful of their purpose and because of their mindfulness, they know *why* they do *what* they do, as Silberman (1970) noted. Their classrooms and schools are not governed by happenstance, trivial, or fleeting interests. Their decisions are driven neither by what the latest educational fad portends, nor by remaining wedded to repeating what they've done in the past simply because "we've always done it that way."

Instead, excellent educators struggle day-in and day-out to reach their students and to build an authentic learning community. They not only muster all of their management skills, interpersonal skills, and technological skills to enable their students and one another to commence forth from their classrooms and schools as more mature and fully functioning human beings. But, more to the point, excellent educators also communicate what the school values, conveying to their students and one another what membership in this special community entails.

The distinction Sergiovanni (1995) has drawn between good and excellent educators generically applies to teachers and administrators in every sector. Whether they practice their craft in public or private schools, good educators struggle to insure that their schools and classrooms are well organized. They work at developing the kinds of interpersonal relations that promote understanding and learning, and they make good curricular choices. They also select instructional activities that encourage maximal student engagement in learning. But, what separates excellent educators from good educators is that the former are ever mindful of their purpose for being in their school and its classrooms. They strive with all of their ability to elevate the moral and intellectual caliber of what will be the next generation's adult citizens.

In sum, Sergiovanni's (1995) model suggests that the symbolic and cultural roles associated with educational excellence build upon three fundamental competencies. "Deliberative" educators (opposed to "rote" instructors) are those teachers and administrators who model for their students and one another the type of person they are all attempting to become, while at the same time marshaling all available skills and resources to inculcate this ideal throughout their school. Together with their students, excellent educators engage in the hard work of forming an educational community steeped in these inspiring ideals and values.

Sergiovanni's (1995) notion that educational excellence is constructed upon the bedrock of educational competence provides a normative framework that can be used by administrators and teachers to design faculty meetings, staff development, and in-service programs. For example, an administrator might first begin by inviting a faculty member to conduct an informal audit to determine the average amount of time spent at faculty meetings that has been devoted to problem-solving, especially those recurring management, interpersonal, and pedagogical problems that never seem to disappear. This percentage might be compared to the average amount of time spent at faculty meetings where substantive issues, like the school's purpose and identity, receive thoughtful attention.

This informal audit might reveal that the community of educators is devoting an inordinate amount of time to routine problem-solving and is failing to seize the opportunity to undertake a pathway toward excellence by becoming more attentive to the school's symbolic and cultural purposes. Focusing faculty meetings, staff development, and in-service programs upon these forces would challenge teachers and administrators to realize that educating youth requires being mindful about what it is

Excellence involves relating what one does to the school's fundamental purpose. Catholic educators might begin by inquiring:
- *Why have I chosen to be in this particular school?*
- *In what ways does the school's purpose challenge me?*
- *How is this school a better place because I minister here?*
- *What might I do to make my school and classroom a better learning environment?*

they are doing from the very first moment they enter the school each and every day. Then, given the comfort of time and continuous progress in learning about what educating youth truly entails, a fundamentally competent faculty can be motivated to coordinate their efforts toward the goal of becoming excellent educators by engaging one another in conversations about these two important dimensions of their profession. Ultimately, they will have learned to work together to provide their students the type of unified educational experience that inculcates the values and ideals which serve as the inspiring purpose for the school's existence (Sergiovanni, 1994).

• excellence and the vocation of the catholic educator...

As was noted earlier, good and excellent teachers and administrators are present in all types of schools. However, for Catholic educators, the symbolic and cultural roles are what distinguish their vocation and work from their colleagues in other sectors (see #4 and #5 in Figures 1 and 2, compare with Figure 3).

Catholic educators stand within their school community not only as professionals who have been specially trained to inculcate the knowledge, skills, and values in their students deemed necessary for citizenship in this world. In addition, Catholic educators stand within their school community as symbols of the knowledge, skills, and values that denote citizens of God's kingdom. Catholic teachers and administrators are the disciples, whose faith, hope, and love symbolize to their students and one another the distinctive meaning, purpose, and values defining the Catholic vision of human life. It is this community of faith whom parents and the Church entrust with the mission of communicating Catholic culture to youth.

Figure 3.

THE FIVE FORCES OF CATHOLIC EDUCATIONAL EXCELLENCE
"*Why* we do what we do"

5. *To mediate Catholic culture.*
4. *To communicate moral and intellectual values.*

"*What* we do"
3. *Provide good curriculum and instruction.*
2. *Develop warm, interpersonal relations.*
1. *Manage the school and its classrooms.*

Adapted from: T. J. Sergiovanni. (1995). *The principalship: A reflective-practice perspective* (3rd ed.). Needham Heights, MA: Allyn and Bacon.

Having surveyed a theoretical model that enables us to distinguish between good and excellent educators, we have come to a point in our journey that we can differentiate how the vocation of the Catholic educator differs from that of other educators. But, we have not yet been able to describe precisely what it is that excellence in this vocation entails.

Our reflections now turn to scripture and tradition. In this survey of Catholic educational thought, we shall seek to understand more fully what it is that Catholic educators are called to be for youth. The heritage of faith preserved in these documents will expose us to some inspiring ideals about which every Catholic educator must become more mindful, that is, if they wish to express authentic educational excellence by communicating the Catholic culture through their lives and ministry in schools

Chapter 4

Visions of Excellence for Catholic Educators: A Scriptural Perspective

Metaphors typically used to describe teaching and administering in schools oftentimes liken the work of educating youth to a "job" or a "career" defined by areas of "professional expertise." Given the functionalist ideology these metaphors convey, theological metaphors like "vocation" and "ministry" may strike many as a somewhat odd and curious way to talk about educating youth.

Sergiovanni's (1995) notion of educational excellence, however, provides a theoretical perspective to reflect upon and describe the substantive purpose motivating the efforts of teachers and administrators. It is this purpose that elevates the work of educating youth to a very challenging and demanding "vocation" and "ministry." Compared to functionalist metaphors, these theological metaphors not only convey a richer understanding about what Catholic educators do, but why they do it in the first place.

To fulfill the demands of this very challenging ministry, Catholic educators build upon the bedrock of skills associated with good educational practice. They manage their classrooms and schools well, communicate meaningfully with one another as well as with all of their students, and they master the technology of their craft, i.e., curriculum and instruction. It is from this basis of competence, Sergiovanni (1995) reminds us, that good educators become excellent educators as they strive to fulfill the substantive purpose at the heart of their profession.

For Catholic educators, however, good educational practice in itself is not enough. In addition, Catholic educators must also convey the assumptions, beliefs, and values representing Catholic culture, as these have been transmitted throughout the Christian centuries in scripture and tradition. Like parents, who are the first educators of youth, Catholic educators are challenged to translate Catholic culture into their interpersonal relations, modeling for their students what is true about human existence and citizenship in this world as well as the next.

Catholic educators, then, express excellence and fulfill the demands of their vocation as they minister to the authentic needs of youth. Their work is not only a job, a profession requiring specialized expertise; it is also divine calling, that is, a ministry requiring courage and confidence. While their task involves providing students the moral and

---

Assign percentages indicating the amount of time you engage in the following activities as you prepare for a new academic year:

- Managerial and organizational matters:
  _____%

- Collaborating with your colleagues:
  _____%

- Studying professional literature to improve curriculum and instruction:
  _____%

- Studying the school's philosophy and mission statement:
  _____%

- Taking time to be alone and to reflect about what you need to do to fulfill the demands of your ministry:
  _____%

What does your list suggest about your priorities as a Catholic educator? Using Sergiovanni's model, are you targeting goodness or excellence?

intellectual knowledge, experiences, and skills that will enable them to function effectively as the next generation's adults, their ministry requires Catholic educators to stand before their students as living witnesses, symbols of God's and the Church's personal interest in their lives.

What vision does scripture offer Catholic educators about their vocation and ministry? In what follows, we will sketch out a scriptural perspective, seeking to understand *why* Catholic educators do *what* they do. These biblical reflections offer Catholic teachers and administrators a theological framework for being mindful about why they do what they do.

Scriptural Reflections — Called, Commissioned, Sent, Empowered

The Christian scriptures are rich with narratives that vividly portray Jesus as a masterful teacher. In one very familiar scene, Jesus is depicted teaching a huge crowd from the mountainside. Another scene places Jesus in the Temple, challenging the authority of false teachers. And, in yet another familiar scene, Jesus calls his disciples aside to a private place where he instructs them about membership in God's kingdom. Of all the images the evangelists invoked to portray Jesus' life and mission, this image of "Jesus the Rabbi" (i.e., Jesus the Teacher) is unquestionably one that has deeply penetrated Christian consciousness throughout the centuries (Pelikan, 1985).

For educators, in particular, the image of "Jesus the Teacher" is perhaps the most powerful and eloquent image for them to reflect upon their life and work as teachers and administrators. However, instead of focusing upon the facts related in these narratives about "*what*" Jesus taught, our attention will turn to the scriptural narratives where Jesus commissioned his disciples to go forth and to teach all nations. Examining some elements of these narratives, we shall endeavor to understand the "*why*" that is the heart of what Jesus' disciples teach: the nature of their call, what it is that they are commissioned to do, where they are sent, and how God has empowered them to proclaim His Word.

These reflections will form a scriptural perspective concerning the vocation of the Catholic educator. It is this perspective that will enable teachers and administrators to differentiate between their "work" and their "vocation," that is, *what* they do and *why* they do it.

• in the Gospel of Mark...

The conclusion of Mark's gospel is the first narrative we shall examine. Commonly referred to as the "commissioning scene," Mark's conclusion has been cherished through the Christians generations, particularly as it has been invoked by preachers to recall the moment when

Scripture is one means by which the heritage of the Catholic faith is transmitted from one generation to the next.
- *In your professional training, was it ever suggested that—or demonstrated how—the bible can serve as a resource for you to reflect upon and evaluate your professional practice ?*
- *Have you ever used biblical narratives to reflect upon your life and work as an educator or to speak with other educators and students about how they might approach problems they have shared with you?*
- *Can you demonstrate how your educational decision-making is related to perspectives about educating youth provided by scripture?*

Jesus' sent his disciples to go forth and to make disciples of all nations. Mark (16:14-20) relates this scene as follows:

14 Afterwards while the Eleven were at table [Jesus] appeared to them and reproached them for their incredulity and dullness, because they had not believed those who had seen him after he was raised from the dead.
15 Then he said to them: "Go forth to every part of the world, and proclaim the Good News to the whole creation.
16 Those who believe it and receive baptism will find salvation; those who do not believe will be condemned.
17 Faith will bring with it these miracles: believers will cast out devils in my name and speak in strange tongues;
18 if they handle snakes or drink any deadly poison, they will come to no harm; and the sick on whom they lay their hands will recover."
19 So after talking with them the Lord Jesus was taken up into heaven, and he took his seat at the right hand of God;
20 but they went out to make their proclamation everywhere, and the Lord worked with them and confirmed their words by the miracles that followed. (NEB)

As this narrative unfolds (v. 14), the Lord Jesus is not happy; in fact, His first act is to reprimand the Eleven for steadfastly refusing to believe Mary of Magdala and the "two of them" (presumably Peter and John) who had brought back the good news that Jesus was raised from the dead. Not possessing the depth of faith that would enable them to believe what had to be for them a rather bizarre sophomoric tale, the Eleven chose instead to dwell upon what human reason dictated must be the facts: Jesus had been crucified, died, and was buried. Given this testimony, the Eleven simply had to deal with their grief and get on with their lives. Persisting in their disbelief, however, the Eleven had unwittingly locked themselves within the confines of a pessimistic attitude that made it impossible for them to see the truth being proclaimed in their midst.

At this point, Mark introduces an important theme. The Lord Jesus, the Risen One, miraculously cuts through all of the physical, psychological, and theological barriers erected by the Eleven. As He suddenly bursts into their midst and stands before them, the Lord Jesus shatters their pessimistic delusions and reprimands the Eleven for their disbelief. He then sends them forth to proclaim the Good News.

As Mark relates this scene, belief in the Resurrection is the heart of the Christian vocation and mission. Only an abiding faith in God's saving power makes it possible for human beings to transcend the limits of human reason, to experience God's gift of salvation, and to be empowered to proclaim the Good News.

Interestingly, the Lord Jesus did not tell the Eleven to return to their lives and their work. Nor did He tell them to remain in their towns, neighborhoods, and surrounding countryside. Instead, the Lord Jesus challenged the Eleven to push beyond their familiar and comfortable status quo, enjoining them to journey into alien territory. Not only were they to go forth to their own people, Mark wrote, the Eleven were also "proclaim the Good News to the whole creation" (v. 15). There were no territorial limits imposed upon their proclamation. They were to proclaim this message to all nations and all peoples.

Theologically, this was a revolutionary message. Commanding the Eleven to go forth to every part of the world and to proclaim the Good News to all people, the Lord Jesus shattered the parochial boundaries of traditional Jewish theology, which had taught that only faithful Jews could be God's Chosen People. This command to teach was, in reality, a commission to invite all people to enter into full communion as members of God's family.

And, Mark reminds us, this teaching would have miraculous effects. The Eleven would cast out devils and speak strange tongues. They would also handle snakes, drink deadly poison, and heal the sick (vv. 17-18). In sum, their teaching would challenge men and women to be courageous by having faith in the Lord Jesus, not simply as an historical personage but, more importantly, as God's living presence active in their midst. Additionally, the Eleven would teach with authority: they would vanquish evil.

Is Mark's account a far-fetched tale? Not for educators who have faith and are mindful of their purpose for being in classrooms and schools.

These teachers and administrators know that the Lord Jesus ministers through them as they challenge their students to reject sin and to accept the responsibilities of membership in God's kingdom. These educators also allow the Lord Jesus, present in and working through them, to speak those "strange tongues" that move young men and women to reject sin, to turn to the Gospel, and to be saved. These educators know, too, that as they help their students confront the oftentimes disconcerting intellectual, psychological, biological, social, and spiritual problems that overwhelm them as they mature, it is the Lord Jesus who handles the metaphorical "snakes" menacing youth. Faith in the Risen One reminds these teachers and administrators, too, that they can drink in, without harm, any poisonous venom sometimes spewed by students whose lives have been deeply shaken or wounded by tragedy. From this evidence, it is clear that these educators teach with divine authority.

The Marcan narrative reminds Catholic educators that what they do is important. They are called, commissioned, and empowered to proclaim the Good News. But, of far greater significance is *why* Catholic educators do what they do: they allow the Lord to minister through them and to perform these miracles exhibiting courageous love. It is their faith in the Lord Jesus that elevates the daily work of educating youth from a mundane job to a ministry of inestimable love.

Relating scripture and your practice:
- *What needs do you believe God is calling you to meet in the people He has sent you to serve?*
- *Identify a "miracle" you experienced occurring through your ministry.*
- *What might your faculty do to focus upon and share their miraculous stories so as to nourish one another's faith?*

For many educators, it is much easier to be devoted to teaching and administering when their professional responsibilities include only those problems directly related to developing and maintaining competence in school and classroom management, human relations, and pedagogy. Sadly though, when educating youth becomes stripped of its scriptural foundations, the words and actions of educators increasingly become rote, emerging not from one's soul, but conditioned by formal and informal contracts, codes of conduct, and "teacher-proofed" curricula. Their "vocation" becomes a "job." Like the Eleven, perhaps it is easier for educators to persist in disbelief, to lock themselves into a comfortable routine, to refuse their call to proclaim the Good News, and to go about their work than it is to listen to God's call and to respond to it through their hard labor.

However, when teachers and administrators exercise mindfulness of what is the heart of their vocation and direct all of their managerial, interpersonal, and professional skills toward fulfilling the Lord's command to teach the Good News, that teaching and administering becomes a vocation. Theirs is a call from the Lord Jesus to proclaim the Good News and to act in His name. For those educators who accept this mission, Mark reminds them: the Lord Jesus will work with and confirm their words by the miracles which follow (v. 20).

Mark's narrative reminds Catholic educators that educational excellence emerges as God speaks to youth through all that teachers and administrators do. Catholic educators are the men and women God has called and commissioned to proclaim His saving word. The primary scriptural challenge to Catholic educators, Mark asserts, is for educators to be freed of any vestiges of disbelief which suggest that the Risen One cannot and does not send Himself through His disciples to proclaim God's saving word to youth.

Faith in the Lord Jesus is the heart of the Catholic educator's vocation. The question Mark places before Catholic educators is: Do you believe this and make it the foundation of your work in schools?

When you were hired to teach or administer:

- *Were the terms of employment described primarily in the "what" you were being asked to do? Or, was your work in the school related to "why you do what you do," that is, your vocation as a Catholic educator?*
- *When you were first introduced to the school community, were you "commissioned" to go forth and to participate in the mission that all educators in the school shared?*
- *Devise ways these biblical images can be translated into practice so that the scriptural foundations of the educator's vocation will be made more explicit to all members of your school community. For example, how might the interview process or the evaluation process be shaped by these biblical images?*

• in the Gospel of Matthew...

Matthew's narrative about the commissioning (28:16-20) offers two additional perspectives concerning discipleship, particularly as these concern the vocation of the Catholic educator.

Matthew reported the scene as follows:

16 The eleven disciples made their way to Galilee, to the mountain where Jesus had told them to meet him.
17 When they saw him, they fell prostrate before him, though some were doubtful.
18 Jesus then came up and spoke to them. He said: "Full authority in heaven and on earth has been committed to me.
19 Go forth therefore and make all nations my disciples; baptize [people] everywhere in the name of the Father and the Son and the Holy Spirit, and teach them to observe all that I have commanded you.
20 And be assured, I am with you always, to the end of time." (NEB)

In this pericope, Matthew sounds very much like Mark, namely, Matthew stresses that the Lord Jesus possesses the full authority of His Father. Second, Matthew reminds his readers that the Eleven are commissioned to make disciples of all nations by baptizing them and teaching them to observe all that the Lord Jesus had commanded. Third, as the Eleven go forth into all the world to proclaim His word, they have the assurance that the Lord Jesus is with them.

Matthew's narrative, however, emphasizes the notion that the source of the disciple's call and the commission to teach emanates from God. For educators who live in nations where the authority to teach and administer is granted by public bodies that certify educators, it is not surprising that state-mandated certification requirements oftentimes receive greater attention than does the call and commission to teach and administer. Matthew reminds Catholic educators, however, that the source of their authority is not defined by a credential. Instead, their authority is a gift God entrusts to those He calls and commissions to educate youth.

Matthew also stresses the notion that fidelity to the Gospel is what characterizes authentic teaching. Because the disciples formed in this generation become the teachers who will proclaim the Good News in the next generation, Catholic educators, like the Eleven, bear the immense responsibility to teach as Jesus did. In short, their teaching is authentic to the degree it emerges, like the Lord's, from a living relationship with the Father. It must be God Who dwells in educators and teaches authoritatively through them.

Matthew's commissioning scene asserts, then, that the primary challenge to Catholic educators is that they allow their relationship with God to be the focus of and to permeate what they do. Being good teachers or administrators is not enough. For Catholic educators, a vital

Oftentimes during their first few weeks on the job, teachers and administrators feel a need to assert their authority.
- *Can you identify an instance where a student or a fellow educator has come to speak with you about a personal matter? What reason(s) were given for selecting you?*
- *In this instance, did you feel a need to assert your authority? Or, were you more attentive to what was needed of you in that particular situation?*
- *What might this situation suggest about the source of the Catholic educator's authority?*

and living relationship with God is the foundation of their authority to teach and administer. This relationship is the substantive purpose at the heart of what they do.

• in the Gospel of John…

The evangelist John (20:19-23) offers yet another version of the commissioning scene:

19 Late that Sunday evening, when the disciples were together behind locked doors, for fear of the Jews, Jesus came and stood among them. "Peace be with you!" he said, and then showed them his hands and his side.
20 So when the disciples saw the Lord, they were filled with joy.
21 Jesus repeated, "Peace be with you!", and said, "As the Father sent me, so I send you."
22 Then he breathed on them, saying, "Receive the Holy Spirit!
23 If you forgive any [one] sins, they stand forgiven; if you pronounce them unforgiven, unforgiven they remain." (NEB)

While the events reported John's commissioning narrative vary dramatically from those recorded by Mark and Matthew, John's narrative provides an additional perspective into the nature of Christian discipleship, particularly the vocation of the educator-disciple. For John, just as the Father sent His Son to proclaim God's saving message, so too, the Lord Jesus breathes the Holy Spirit into His disciples so that they might fulfill their call to proclaim the Good News.

In this narrative, John focuses neither upon the disciples' disbelief nor the miraculous evidence that will accompany their ministry. Neither does he highlight authoritative teaching or the disciple's relationship with the Father. In contrast to the images of the Marcan and Matthean texts, John maintains that discipleship is related to the power of the Holy Spirit. It is the Holy Spirit Who provides testimony to the fact that the Lord Jesus continues to work effectively through His disciples.

How is the Holy Spirit manifested in the disciples' lives?

For John, the answer is simple: these disciples are empowered by the Holy Spirit to lift what burdens their brothers and sisters (20:23). The power of the Holy Spirit, dwelling in the disciples, is what enables them to forgive sins and to restore men and women to the life God has given them in creating them as His children. Empowered by the Holy Spirit, these disciples lift-up what weighs down people so that they might rise-up to the freedom that can be theirs as God's sons and daughters.

This Johannine perspective suggests that the vocation of the Catholic educator is very much linked to the ministry of healing. The primary work of teaching and administering in schools is not only educational; it is, more importantly, the work of helping youth to reclaim

Catholic educators bear witness to Christ and are empowered by His spirit.
- *Do you believe that God has called you to be a Catholic educator?*
- *Enumerate what you have given up to respond to God's call.*
- *In your work as a Catholic educator, when do you most experience Christ at work within you?*
- *Identify an experience when your prayer was one of thankfulness to God for having invited you to participate in the saving mystery of Christ.*

> *Through their ministry, Catholic educators lift the burdens experienced by others.*
> • *Reflect upon your experience as a Catholic educator. Can you relate instances where you helped others resolve problems that were burdening them?*

that quality of life where they experienced the freedom that was theirs as sons and daughters of God. The vocation of the Catholic educator, then, is a prophetic ministry, one where educators spend themselves in the challenging work of freeing youth from the power of evil weighing them down. These educators view their primary work as healing the evils resulting from sin and offering youth the gift of salvation.

• in the Book of Acts...

In light of John's testimony, some Catholic educators might be wondering: "When will the Holy Spirit come to effect these marvelous things?" The Book of Acts responds directly to this question, reporting that Jesus told His disciples, "It is not for you to know about dates or times, which the Father has set within his own control. But you will receive power when the Holy Spirit comes upon you; and you will bear witness for me in Jerusalem, and all over Judaea and Samaria, and away to the ends of the earth" (Acts 1:7-8, NEB).

The author of Acts, sounding like John, argues that it is not time (the "when") that should be primary for disciples. Rather, they should focus upon the presence of the Lord Jesus, here and now, through what they do. Prescient knowledge of the day and time of the Lord's return is not the focus for those whose abiding faith in the Lord Jesus reminds them that He continues to be present. Through the power of the Holy Spirit, the Lord's disciples receive the power to act in His name and place until the end of the world.

The biblical imperative is clear: the vocation of the Catholic educator is a challenge to effect the reality of God's kingdom here and now, not in some distant or hoped-for future. For Catholic educators, it is not good enough to fantasize or hope about what might be done for their students, only to return to their classrooms and schools, frustrated and despairing that nothing can be done. As the disciples of the Lord Jesus, Catholic educators are called to intervene in their student's lives or evil manifests its power.

Catholic educators do this, not because they are trained specialists, but because they have faith that the Lord is present with them. The salvation that has been promised is brought to fulfillment here and now because they teach the Good News authoritatively in the name and place of the Risen Lord.

• summary: the vocation of the Catholic educator— scriptural reflections...

The scriptural texts we have surveyed provide a variety of perspectives for Catholic educators to reflect upon their vocation and to think about how their work in schools might express their vocation more authoritatively. Each text has provided a unique perspective that, when examined in combination with the others, forms a rich portrait identifying the authentic disciple.

This portrait suggests, first, that the disciple is called by the Lord Jesus. It is within the context of this divine summons that the Lord commissions and sends His disciples into the world to proclaim the Good News. This portrait also suggests that discipleship involves more than being called, commissioned, and sent. In addition, disciples are empowered by the Holy Spirit to forgive sins and, in doing so, to restore life and to make disciples of all people until the end of time. Through each disciple's ministry, the Lord's message continues to be proclaimed in each generation as new disciples respond generously to their call to teach all nations.

For me, one of the most powerful ideas embedded in these texts relates to the disciples' mission. The Lord Jesus does not call His disciples to devote their lives to contemplative introspection and solitary prayer. Instead, the Lord sends His disciples into the real world. They must be "active contemplatives," men and women who share an intimate relationship with their Father, but at the same time, discover their fulfillment as they proclaim the Good News to real people with real needs and oftentimes very real problems. Their mission is to offer men and women the healing unction of the Holy Spirit.

These scriptural foundations provide a normative framework for reflecting upon what authentic discipleship requires. For those disciples God calls to educate youth, the crucial requirement concerns whether they press beyond rote, immediate decision-making into the realm of deliberative inquiry into mission for which they have come together in their school. As disciples, Catholic educators engage in deliberate, moral decision-making steeped in the fact that these disciples have been called by God to "Teach as Jesus Did" (National Conference of Catholic Bishops, 1972, 1984). Through their collective words and actions (*what* they do), teachers and administrators symbolize for one another and their students the living presence of the Risen Lord (*why* they do what they do). These disciples communicate the culture of God's kingdom, embodied for all generations in the Good News.

In the next section, our focus will turn from reflecting upon scripture to Church tradition, particularly as this tradition concerned educational matters during the 19th and 20th centuries. Specifically, we will concentrate upon the Church's thought as it identified the pressing need for local Catholic communities to provide for their children's moral and intellectual formation in an increasingly utilitarian milieu. Finally, we shall consider what this implies for Catholic educators, especially as these ideas have been elaborated during the past two centuries in the context of the U.S. Catholic community.

Because what follows in the next three sections is intended to

> *Scripture offers insights into the spirituality of the Catholic educator.*
> - *What might teachers and administrators in your school do to focus more effectively upon the scriptural foundations of their call?*
> - *How might educators be commissioned so that every member of your school community would better understand their call and what it means to teach as Jesus did?*
> - *What might the scriptural foundations of the vocation of the Catholic educator imply for evaluating teachers and administrators?*
> - *How might annual evaluation be made into a formative experience, focusing educators upon their vocation?*

familiarize readers with primary materials from Church tradition, some readers may find it more suitable for their purposes to skip over the detailed textual analysis to the summary provided at the end of each of the next three sections. An overview of this tradition is also provided as an introduction to our reflections concerning very practical matters, that is, the theological virtues and their implications for Catholic educational practice.

Visions of Excellence for Catholic Educators: Theological Perspectives from the Pre-Vatican II Church (1800-1960)

The scriptural narratives reporting the disciples' commissioning remind Catholic educators how the Christian community has, from its earliest days, maintained an intense interest in educating its members about the Good News. Teaching the faith has been and will continue to be a primary endeavor of the Christian community. These scriptural narratives also remind Catholic educators that their vocation is of paramount significance for the Church's future: they are the disciples who have been delegated the immense responsibility to form the next generation's disciples.

For the first fifteen Christian centuries, the Church's general attitude toward educating youth paralleled that of Western culture. This attitude gradually began to change during the Counter-Reformation era, and especially during and after the Enlightenment, when democratic forms of government began to emerge and utilitarian philosophies began to take hold in discourse about educational matters. Eventually, as civil authorities began to mandate that religious education be excluded from state-supported schools during the early 19th century, the Church became embroiled in a bitter debate, one that continues even today, concerning what educational program is best for youth.

Although the acrimony engendered in the debate has been unfortunate, pitting civil authorities against Church leaders, perhaps it was fortuitous, educationally speaking, because both parties to this debate have focused upon the important role educators undertake in the educational process. For civil authorities, educators are agents of a secular state, that is, specialists hired because they have received training in how to best convey to youth the knowledge, skills, and values required if they are to be able to fulfill their civic responsibilities when they became adult citizens. In contrast, Church leaders have used a very different set of lenses to view educators: these men and women are the critical linchpin in providing youth an "authentic" educational program, that is, a moral and an intellectual formation that will enable youth to exercise their responsibilities as adult citizens not only of this world but also as members of God's kingdom. Each of these two contrasting views have profound implications for educational practice.

> *Along with scripture, documents of the "teaching" Church (i.e., its magisterium) are a second means by which the Catholic culture is transmitted from one generation to the next.*
>
> - *In your professional training, was it ever suggested that—or demonstrated how—Church tradition can serve as a resource for you to reflect upon and evaluate your professional practice?*
> - *Have you ever used Church teaching to reflect upon your life and work as an educator or to speak with other people about how they might approach problems they have shared with you?*
> - *Can you identify how "what you do" as an educator is related to perspectives about educating youth conveyed by the Church's tradition?*
> - *In view of these facts, do you believe your profession is more of a "job" or a "vocation"?*

With this general introduction to a very complex and intricate history, we turn now to a detailed examination of Church documents issued during two eras, that of the pre-Vatican II Church (c. 1800-1960) and that of the post-Vatican II Church (c. 1960-1990). These are not two dichotomous periods demarcating trends in the Church's thinking about educational matters. Rather, this tradition is developmental in nature, for it was during these two eras that the Church formulated a theological rationale concerning the education of youth, laid the foundation that clarified the vocation of the Catholic educator, and promoted an educational vision that described education as "formation" rather than mere "instruction."

• in the mid-19th century...

The vocation of the Catholic educator began to emerge as a distinct theme in Church documents at least as early as mid-19th century Europe, when nation-states began to enact educational legislation that excluded religious instruction from state-supported schools.

Taken at face value, the rationale embodied in the legislation is straight-forward: the education of youth is *public* matter and, hence, subject to state regulation. As far as the state's interest in educating youth is concerned, the issue concerns practical utility, that is, how the state can best provide youth the knowledge, skills, and values they will need to exercise their civic responsibilities as adult citizens.

Embedded in this rationale, however, is a fundamental change in how the relationship between parents, the Church, and the state are to be configured, especially as this relationship concerns educating youth. In the socio-political context where these three parties actively cooperate (as, for example, when there is a state religion or when a government supports private schools), parental interests are provided for as the Church and state work together to furnish youth the educational program that parents desire for their children. But, when a state legislates educational matters, in particular, when religious education is to be excluded from state-supported schools, civil authorities usurp parental or Church interests (or both), compelling them to be subservient to the state's interest. That is, unless parents have the economic means to opt out of state-supported schools and to send their children to private schools.

One of the first challenges to governmental hegemony in the education of youth is contained in a letter Pius IX (1864, 1979) wrote to the Archbishop of Fribourg. In that letter, the Pope lashed out against those "perverse" philosophies excluding educators and religious authorities from defending the integrity of faith in governmental schools. For Pius IX, the problem (i.e., how to best provide youth an education) drew attention away from the fundamental principle at stake in the argument (i.e., whether any government had the right in matters concerning the education of youth to subject parental and Church interests to its absolute control).

For Pius IX, religion was not a strictly *private* matter, as those who advocated the secularization of public education maintained. Instead, the Pope maintained that religion is an eminently *public* matter, one which informs adults about their moral responsibilities as citizens. For Pius IX, the legislation being enacted did not simply exclude religious education from schools. This legislation was, in fact, a frontal assault upon parental and Church interests in educating youth and the role that religion should play in discourse about public issues. If schools did not provide youth a serious program of moral formation, students would be inculcated in a secularized atmosphere that would fail to equip them with the moral referent they would to exercise their rights and responsibilities not only as adult citizens of a secular nation, but more importantly, as citizens of God's kingdom.

While Pius IX was contesting the secularization of school curricula on the European continent, quite the opposite situation was emerging in the United States as public school boards were mandating a pan-Protestant program of religious education for students attending public schools (Tyack & Hansot, 1982). Unfortunately, civility did not always prevail. Lannie and Diethorn (1968) have chronicled how, in Philadelphia, Bishop Kenrick saw tempers flare and destructive riots ensue because Catholic students in public schools were being required to read scripture from the Protestant bible and to sing Protestant hymns. In New York, even though civility prevailed for the most part, Lannie and Diethorn exposed how Bishop Hughes utilized every political lever at his disposal to exercise his episcopal prerogatives.

In the end, however, both bishops had unwittingly thrust themselves into the unenviable position having to champion the cause of excluding religious instruction from public schools so that Catholic youth would not be indoctrinated into Protestantism. Thus, in what is perhaps one of the most ironic twists in Catholic educational history, while Pius IX was arguing against civil authorities in the Old World who wanted religious education excluded from the school curriculum, Bishops Kenrick and Hughes were arguing against civil authorities in the New World who wanted religious education (albeit a nondenominational program) included in the public school curriculum!

As this controversy was reaching a fevered pitch, Pius IX (1875, 1979) entered the fray with an instruction addressed to the U.S. hierarchy. In it, the Pope maintained that public schools which excluded religious education were "intrinsically dangerous" because youth would grow up without any appreciation for the role that religion plays as it relates to the exercise of their civic duties. To remedy this proximate danger to the faith and morals of youth, a danger that "borders on perversion," Pius IX argued that Catholic parents need to realize that the

> *As secularism spread during the 19th century, the intellectual formation of youth began to gain ascendancy over their religious formation. Only one century later:*
> - *Was your pre-service training concerned with educating the student's moral as well as intellectual capacity?*
> - *When you were hired, was your vision of religious formation for students discussed, challenged, or affirmed?*
> - *In your daily work, do you find yourself preoccupied more with providing your students a moral or intellectual formation? Which do you feel students need most?*
> - *Has your continuing education focused primarily upon the moral (vocational) issues or instructional (professional) involved in educating youth?*
> - *What professional challenges do these type of questions raise for you?*

preservation of the Catholic faith is a matter of utmost urgency. And, if necessary, the Pope mandated that Catholic schools be constructed so that Catholic youth would be exposed to subject matter in a way that would be conversant with and reflect Catholic principles of teaching and morality.

In retrospect, Pius IX's vision was prophetic: he foresaw the threat that secularizing the school curriculum posed to youth. But, with his options limited to the bully-pulpit of the papacy, all the Pope could really hope to accomplish was to exhort the Catholic hierarchy to be more mindful of and to exercise more forcefully their moral rights. And, in those societies where governments had already intruded upon parental and ecclesiastical rights (e.g., the United States), all Pius IX could hope to accomplish was to prevail upon parents to send their children to Catholic schools in those places where they had already been established or to build separate Catholic schools where there weren't any.

For the U.S. Catholic community, Pius IX may best be remembered for the fact that his instruction laid the foundation for the hierarchy to legislate building Catholic schools, which it did nine years later at the Third Baltimore Council in 1884. For Catholic educators, however, Pius IX's legacy involves how he foresaw and predicted the effects a secularized curriculum would have upon youth and, as these young men and women came to exercise their public responsibilities as adult citizens, the harmful effect secularization would have upon nations.

Pius IX's viewpoint hinged upon the notion that teachers and administrators are in schools not merely to convey the secular knowledge, skills, and values that youth will need to exercise their civic responsibilities as adult citizens. For Pius IX, educators fulfill a far more substantive purpose. In schools, educators are parental delegates, teachers and administrators, who bear the responsibility to make their classrooms and schools places where youth receive the moral and intellectual formation that parents want for their sons and daughters.

Even today, Pius IX's challenge to Catholic educators continues to be relevant: What does the secularization of American public education imply for parents and their delegates? What are their moral obligations to youth?

• in the late-19th century...

Leo XIII (who succeeded Pius IX and reigned from 1878-1903) further refined Church teaching in matters concerning the education of youth. It was not until the ninth year of his pontificate, however, that Leo XIII issued *Officio sanctissimo* (1887, 1979), an encyclical setting forth the Church's view about the educational rights and responsibilities of parents, the Church, and the state. In an era, like ours, when there exists much confusion about rights and responsibilities in educational matters, *Officio* presents a good summary to reflect upon the proper relationship between parental, Church, and state interests. In addition, *Officio* provides educators a well-reasoned philosophical and theological basis for reflecting upon their ministry.

In *Officio*, Leo XIII outlined what had become by the late 19th century the traditional notion about parental, Church, and state interests as they concern the education of youth. Parents, for their part, bear a divine obligation to educate their children in matters of faith and morals. This obligation stems from their role as co-creators with God of their children. Because parental interests in the education of youth are divine in origin, they supersede all other interests.

For its part, the Church, too, bears an interest in educating youth, although its interest is secondary to parental interests. As a divine institution charged with the duty to teach the Good News to all nations, the Church is obliged to support parents in their efforts to provide their children a moral formation. The Church is especially obligated to assert its interest when, for example, states compel parents to send their children to schools that do not provide a moral formation. In the more grave situation where, for example, parents are negligent in discharging their educational responsibility or do not really understand what their duty is, the Church's interest supersedes parental interests because their negligence presents a proximate danger to the faith and morals of youth.

Leo XIII also upheld the notion that the state possesses an interest, albeit a secondary interest, in educating youth, for, he reasoned, an educated citizenry ultimately advances and perfects the state. But, the Pope argued, a state cannot limit its interest solely to the sphere of the intellect. In addition, Leo XIII insisted, the state's best interest is served when youth also receive a moral formation. One consequence implicit in this line of reasoning is that the state ultimately bears the obligation to assist parents as they seek to provide a moral education for their children.

When the educational interests of parents, the Church, and the state coalesce, as they do in Catholic schools, Leo XIII reaffirmed, youth receive a "true" education. This educational program unites both natural and revealed truths which, in turn, promote authentic human freedom. Such an outcome is possible, however, only when learning is placed at the service of the faith (Leo XIII, 1897, 1979).

Though *Officio sanctissimo* has been overshadowed by Leo XIII's social encyclical, *Rerum Novarum*, *Officio* is an important encyclical for understanding the development of Catholic educational philosophy. It sets forth a philosophical and theological rationale explicating the common duties and interests borne by parents, the Church, and the state as they collaborate in cultivating moral and intellectual perfection in youth. This encyclical also promotes an integrated curriculum, one balancing the demands of faith with those of reason and promoting authentic

Leo XIII identified the ideal relationship that should exist between the three partners involved in educating youth.
- *In what ways do you seek to cooperate actively with parents, envisioning yourself as their delegate?*
- *In light of Leo XIII's vision of parental rights, how might you challenge your colleagues to provide for a more authentic educational experience for youth today?*
- *Identify how the Church and state can best assist you to provide your students the educational program their parents desire.*

freedom. True educators, then, provide their students an educational program integrating those moral and intellectual lessons that are exercised in one's private and public life.

Officio sanctissimo is also an important encyclical because it provides Catholic educators a comprehensive vision of their ministry in schools. As members of two communities (that is, the civic community of their nation and the faith community of their Church) that have distinct interests in educating youth, Catholic educators are called upon to serve and protect three different (and sometimes, conflicting) interests: parents, the Church, and the state. To the degree that Catholic educators are successful in balancing these interests, young men and women receive the moral and intellectual formation that will enable them to exercise their rights and responsibilities as citizens not only of this world but of God's kingdom as well.

• in the early 20th century...

Early in a pontificate that spanned eleven years (1903-1914), Pius X published the encyclical, *On the Teaching of Christian Doctrine* (1905, 1946), in which he stated flatly that even though many Christians possessed abundant secular knowledge, "they live rashly and imprudently with regard to religion" (1905, 1946, pp. 3-4). The situation had become so perverse, he argued, that "the majority of men in our times must be considered uninstructed" (p. 13).

To remedy this troubling situation, Pius X took dead aim at a surprising target: pastors in local parishes. Challenging them not to neglect their obligation to catechize youth, the Pope reminded pastors that their preaching must be directed not only toward adults, but more precisely, toward youth. For pastors, Pius X's encyclical set a lofty goal: their preaching should seek to impart in youth Christian faith and morality, encourage in them zeal and ardor for God, and challenge them to live more simple and sincere lives. And, even though "teaching the catechism is unpopular with many because as a rule it is deemed of little account..." (p. 9), the Pope reminded pastors that they should not undertake this ministry without careful study and preparation. In sum, Pius X was telling pastors to hone their catechetical skills:

> They are mistaken who think that, because of inexperience and lack of training of the people, the work of catechizing can be performed in a slipshod fashion. On the contrary, the less educated the hearers, the more zeal and diligence must be used to adapt the sublime truths to their untrained minds; these truths, indeed, far surpass the natural understanding of the people yet must be known by all—the uneducated and the cultured—in order that they may arrive at eternal happiness. (1905, 1946, p. 14)

Educators teach by their words as well as by their actions.

- *How are your words and actions a catechism, instructing youth in authentic Christian conduct?*
- *When you see a student or fellow educator standing in need of correction, are you willing and able to provide guidance so that these individuals may reform their lives?*
- *Identify a situation where you were willing to accept justified criticism from your students and colleagues.*

While the tone of this encyclical reflects an "us-against-them" mentality, it is sobering to recall that educators in Europe during this era were educating those young men and women who, during the next two generations, would be the adults making the momentous decisions that would ensnare the European continent in two devastating conflagrations. From the perspective of Catholic educational philosophy, Pius X's anti-worldly attitude was, in reality, a prescient theological critique prophetically reading the signs of the times and identifying how a strictly secular education, one devoid of its religious foundation, would unleash a generation of men and women who would know little of their religious and moral responsibility for the world that God had entrusted to their stewardship. Or, perhaps even worse, as was the case in the Nuremberg trials, men who sincerely believed they bore no responsibility for their atrocities, merely because they were following orders.

What Pius X asked of his pastors is, for most educators, something that is simply part-and-parcel of their daily work. At times, their preaching may take the form of an exhortation, entreating students to practice their faith in the conduct of their lives. At other times, educators may preach in expository form, alerting students to the dangers posed by their moral blindness. Whenever Catholic educators mount their pulpit and preach Christian morality, they are catechizing youth, exhorting them to embrace the Good News by turning away from sin and expressing virtuous behavior through all that they say and do.

Maybe, though, some educators believe that it would better to ignore student misbehavior or immorality, leaving that sensitive matter to others to rectify. However, the consequences of failure in preaching about fundamental morality are too important for educators to overlook. As Pius X noted, it will be in later generations, when the adults being formed in classrooms and schools today are called upon to make decisions affecting the lives of other human beings (and their nations as well), that the effects of the failure to preach right moral conduct will become evident.

Perhaps Pius X overstated matters, finding himself disturbed by the reports he had received from his legates stationed throughout Europe and the United States. And, then, perhaps he wasn't overstating matters, having taken an objective and critical look at the effects that secularizing educational programs had in the lives of ordinary men and women.

The evidence argues that Pius X read the signs of the times accurately: youth were being deprived of the moral formation they deserved. From the perspective of Catholic educational philosophy, Pius X's anti-worldly attitude was, in reality, a prescient theological critique correctly identifying how a strictly secular education would unleash a generation of men and women who would know little of their public responsibility for the world God had entrusted to their stewardship.

Pius X reminds educators that their vocation requires them, like true pastors of souls, to muster and the perfect all of their catechetical skills so that the moral principles they preach in their classrooms and schools today will prove effective in future generations. The deleterious effects of catechetical malpractice on the part of any generation's educators are simply too high a price for humanity to pay. The vocation of the Catholic educator, then, is to preach to young men and women the Christian vision of human existence and right human conduct. Catholic educators must never underestimate the importance of their role as preachers of the Good News.

• in the second and third decades of the 20th century...

During the second and third decades of the 20th century, Pius XI (1922-1939) synthesized Catholic educational thought in his 1929 encyclical entitled, *On the Christian Education of Youth*. This influential document, popularly known as the "Magna Carta of Catholic Education," provided an eloquent description of the nature and purpose of Catholic education. This papal letter also advanced significant theological reflections concerning the vocation of the Catholic educator.

In the words of Pius XI:

> Perfect schools are the result not so much of good methods as of good teachers, teachers who are thoroughly prepared and well-grounded in the matter they have to teach; who possess the intellectual and moral qualifications required by their important office; who cherish a pure and holy love for the youths confided to them, because they love Jesus Christ and His Church, of which these are the children of predilection; and who have sincerely at heart the true good of family and country. (1929, p. 48)

Notice that, for Pius XI, the foundation of the educator's vocation is professional competence. Schools simply cannot fulfill their cultural purpose without faculty who possess pedagogical competence. However, as he also pointed out, professional competence is not the desired end. Instead, Pius XI warned, professional competence is only the beginning, a starting point, for developing a truly excellent (or, in his words, "perfect") school.

On the face of it, Pius XI was reminding his global audience that educating youth demands much more than abundant resources and good classroom instruction. This reasoning is delusionary, he suggested, for when an educator's motive emanates from this myopic view of education, focusing as it does solely upon material things, pedagogy cannot be perfected. In contrast, the pontiff asserted, the essential difference demarcating good and excellent educators is discovered by probing their intrinsic motivation. "Perfect schools are the result...of good teachers...who cherish a pure and holy love for the youths confided to them..." (1929, p. 48), Pius XI wrote. It is this intrinsic motive, the vocation of the Catholic educator, that challenges teachers and administrators to surpass a purely materialistic view of education in order that they may offer their students a formative experience of extraordinary and permanent value.

As Catholic educational thought was developing during the first four decades of the 20th century, educational excellence was increasingly being defined to be a consequence of a theological motive: the charity of the Lord Jesus living in and motivating teachers and educators to provide for the moral and intellectual needs of youth. As Christ dwells in the hearts of educators, He inspires a true love of youth, one motivating them to utilize whatever material resources they have, whether these resources are abundant or scarce, to perfect their pedagogical or administrative repertoire for the benefit of youth.

What unites educators and students in excellent schools, then, is not professional competence, earned in a professional training program and verified by an educational credential. What ensnares educators and their students in excellent schools are the bonds of charity. This motive is the heart of the vocation of the Catholic educator. It is not a skill that can be learned, but a God-given grace brought to perfection through love of God and neighbor.

In terms of U.S. Catholic educational history, it is important to recall that the Church was insisting that a theological motive was at the center of educational practice during an era when pervasive efforts were underway to promote the standardization of educational practice (Callahan, 1962). Scientific standards were needed, most educational policymakers argued, to insure that teachers were doing what they were hired to do and schools were achieving what they were designed to achieve. Objective standards and assessments were quickly replacing subjective relationships and evaluations.

Was the Church wrong and were the educational policymakers right? Is the heart of educational excellence found in objective standards and assessments?

Historical evidence substantiates the argument that many Catholic educators were deficient when measured against newly mandated accreditation and certification standards. In fact, they did not have the human or material resources that policymakers had deemed necessary to provide youth the educational program they needed. And, it is true, many local parishes did not have the fiscal resources to provide adequate educational facilities and programs.

Interestingly, however, these uncertificated educators, who practiced their craft in unaccredited schools, provided the moral and intellectual program that enabled the children of Catholic immigrants, in only one generation, to make a vital contribution to the nation's social, eco-

> *During the first-half of the 20th century, papal teaching argued that true educational excellence is defined in terms of charity being the operative core of the educator's work.*
> - *In what ways does this argument challenge notions that "more money" will make schools better?*
> - *How does this papal teaching refocus the identity of the Catholic educator?*
> - *Develop a schema for evaluating Catholic educators steeped in the principles articulated by Pius XI.*

nomic, and military mainstream. This success story contradicts the notion that accreditation standards are inextricably linked to educational excellence. In light of the experience of the Catholic educational community both during the first three decades of the 20th century (and during the post-Vatican II era in urban Catholic schools as well), it is far more plausible to accept Pius XI's assertion: excellence is linked to a theological motive and is achieved when the charity of Christ, the *why*, is expressed through the educator's profession, the *what*. Accreditation standards can only support that theological virtue, not replace it.

The *Christian Education of Youth* also accentuated an important philosophical point in arguing that educators hold an "important office." That is, parents and civil society have delegated to educators important responsibilities necessary to the proper functioning of family and society. Pius XI's pastoral perspective argued that educators serve in the name and place of parents, the Church, and civil society. This office, and the trust incumbent with it, does not cloak the community of educators with a mantle of pre-eminence and immunity in educational matters, nor does it set them apart from those who have entrusted educational matters to them. The principle of subsidiarity is operative here: educators act as trustees in the name and place of the three societies they represent, bearing the sacred trust to make educational decisions that will fulfill parental, ecclesial, and societal interests in the education of youth.

• in the mid-20th century...

As the last pontiff who reigned prior to the Second Vatican Council, Pius XII (1939-1958) expanded upon many of the now-familiar educational themes promulgated by his predecessors. But, more than his predecessors did, Pius XII broadened Church teaching as it concerned the vocation of the Catholic educator.

In a radio message to the Fifth Inter-American Congress on Catholic Education meeting in Havana, Cuba, Pius XII specified four characteristics identifying what are typically called "good" teachers (what were identified earlier in this monograph as "excellent" teachers). It was the fourth characteristic Pius XII cited that spoke specifically about the vocation of the Catholic educator and what it is that these educators truly communicate to students. The Pope said:

> Good teachers, finally, are careful to educate rather than merely to instruct; they are capable, above all, of forming and of molding souls chiefly through contact with their own....To achieve this—We repeat— "be fathers of souls more than propagators of sterile information," form your pupils above all "by the example of your life." (1954b, pp. 483-484)

There is no hypocrisy evident in these disciples; it is their courageous example, a moral quality, that motivates students to want to imitate their teachers' example. It is through the example of their lives that excellent teachers embody all that they teach.

One year later, Pius XII built upon this ideal, arguing that the essence of God's love for youth is communicated within the confines of a very privileged interaction, namely, the relationship that educators forge with their students.

> "Teacher" is the highest title that can be given to an instructor. The teacher's function demands something higher and more profound than the function of the person who merely communicates a knowledge of things. The "teacher" is a person who knows how to create a close relationship between his own soul and the soul of a child. It is he who personally devotes himself to guiding the inexperienced pupil towards truth and virtue. It is he in a word, who molds the pupil's intellect and will so as to fashion as best he can a being of human and Christian perfection. (Pius XII, 1955, p. 514)

Carefully distinguishing between an "instructor" and a "teacher" (as in this monograph we have distinguished "teachers" from "educators"), Pius XII asserted that a particular mode of communication transpires within classrooms and schools, that is, an intimate communication between souls. For educators, it is this particular mode of communication that stimulates students to experience through the teacher's words, acts, and affect, the actual incarnation of God's love. In order to be able to communicate at this profoundly spiritual level, Pius XII wrote, "[t]rue teachers must be complete persons and Christians...imitators of the only Divine Master Jesus Christ" (1955, p. 514), who know their students through observation as well as by talking with and listening to them.

The intimate communication between souls characterized in the educator-student relationship is a grace-filled invitation for educators and students to participate in the school community's substantive purpose. Educators who steep their craft in this theological mission are concerned not merely with functional matters (i.e., transmitting the facts, information, and values that will enable students to function as adult citizens), as important as these are. In schools where educators and students endeavor to speak with one another from their souls, the educational community is also, and perhaps more importantly so, concerned with substantive learnings that include, for example, the moral virtues, like loyalty, courage, devotion to duty, as well as love of family and civil society. In schools where these moral virtues are inspired, practiced, and inculcated, all members receive and continue their education in the substantive matters pertaining not only to citizenship in this world but more importantly in the kingdom of God as well.

By the middle of the 20th century, the vocation of the Catholic

For Pius XII, while "instructors" communicate the content of the curriculum, "teachers" engage in an intimate communication with their students' souls.

- *How might classroom communication become a more effective vehicle to communicate the Catholic community's vision of life?*
- *List ways that Pius XII's ideals offer Catholic educators an insight into the difference between "good" and "excellent" classrooms and schools.*
- *Identify the distinctive purpose of the Catholic educator and how all of the Catholic educator's decision-making can serve school and classroom purposes.*
- *Using Pius XII's ideals, explore what is needed to transform a good Catholic school into an excellent one.*
- *Were administrators, teachers, and students to respond to one another from their souls, enumerate how you believe their school's culture would change.*

educator was recognized not merely as a call to expend one's talents and energies in a secular profession, one where success is assessed through objective measures. For Pius XII, the vocation of the Catholic educator is also a lifestyle steeped in scriptural idealism, an expression of the teaching authority given by Christ to His disciples, as well as the willingness to suffer martyrdom for the benefit of youth. The vocation of the Catholic educator is God's call to the educator's heart, a divine summons to devote one's talents and energies to enable youth to undertake their mission to continue building God's kingdom until that time when the Risen Lord comes to claim God's kingdom.

Catholic educators, then, are generous in their response to God's covenant with His people. These disciples seek to express Gospel ideals and principles as the foundation of a truly good life. They desire to direct their energies to protect youth from the power of evil and are willing to undergo weariness and discomfort to form those who will serve God, Church, and society as adult citizens. As Pius XII (1954a) expressed these ideals,

> [t]here are thousands of adolescents entrusted to you during the delicate years of their development; you have a serious responsibility for the formation of...youth and you are making an important contribution to the preparation of a better future for your country. As Christians, you cannot remain indifferent, as teachers, you have the joy of being able to cooperate effectively in the renewal of your generation. (p. 481)

There is little doubt that competent instruction is necessary for humans to be capable of engaging one another in those important matters related to family and civic life (Hirsch, 1987). But more importantly, it is necessary that educators inculcate moral virtues as a basis for young men and women to recognize and to foster their true dignity. However, as Pius XII's explication of Catholic educational theory and its implications for the vocation of the Catholic educator make clear, authentic moral formation is not indoctrination. Rather, within the context of an intimate conversation between each educator and each student, a relationship characterized by Christian personalism, young men and women come to recognize the Lord Jesus living and acting in their midst.

Through this privileged relationship, rooted as it is in genuine love of neighbor, educators enflame the restless desires of youth to imitate the heroic sanctity of Jesus the Teacher, the Risen Lord embodied in their teachers and administrators. Students who receive this authentic moral formation, Pius XII reminds us, will be the graduates who will be prepared to devote their talent and energy and to serve as the architects of the social restoration and renewal of all things in Christ.

According to Pius XII, the effect Catholic educators have upon their students is to serve as lifelong inspirations. By upholding Gospel ideals, by teaching with the authority of Christ, and by willingly undergoing weariness and discomfort for the young men and women whom they truly love, Catholic educators fulfill their vocation. They witness to the Good News as they provide a perfect moral and intellectual formation for those disciples who will serve God, Church, and society in the next generation. These educators contribute to the common good by erecting a barrier that guards youth as evil manifests itself and threatens them.

• summary: the vocation of the Catholic educator— theological reflections from the pre-Vatican II Church...

During the second-half of the 19th and first-half of the 20th centuries, the Church stood foursquare against the world, especially against what it called "modernism," that is, the secularism, materialism, and moral relativism inherent in post-Enlightenment thought which the Church found particularly repugnant to its view of human existence.

As modernism impacted educational theory, the Church was especially troubled that progressive educational theories had fallen prey to modernism's optimistic promises. Dewey's educational philosophy, for example, exalted the notion of shaping learning environments (1916, 1944), the educational process; traditional Catholic educational philosophy stressed educational ends, that is, what God intends for men and women (Maritain, 1944). The Church warned about the threat modernism posed to authentic human freedom and mustered its moral authority to counteract those trends by articulating a philosophical and theological rationale concerning how to authentically educate youth.

While antimodernism was being enforced by Church authorities, unanimity did not prevail for there were some Catholic intellectuals who sought to merge the best of progressive educational theory with traditional Catholic educational philosophy (Murphy, 1973, 1974). At Catholic University of America, for example, Dr. Thomas Edward Shields engaged his talents in a monumental and largely successful struggle to certify Catholic educators (Wohlwent, 1968), using a synthesis that melded progressive educational theory with traditional Catholic educational philosophy (Shields, 1907). Largely through Dr. Shields' efforts in the Sisters College and Sisters Summer School, multitudes of religious women received their pedagogical training and eventual certification, informed by Dr. Shields' progressivist ideals (Meyers, 1947; Shields, 1919; Ward, 1947).

Especially since the mid-1960s, many have been critical of the Church's stance toward modernism. Much of this criticism, however, has failed to recognize the fact that the Church rightly upheld the principle that education involves forming youth both morally and intellectually, in order that they might be prepared to live truly good lives.

The Church had a legitimate critique, especially as modernism began to exercise hegemony in educational theorizing. Without the balance provided by an authentic moral formation, modernism's materialistic foundations constituted a proximate danger to the faith and morals of youth. And, for the Church, these were issues that should have presented grave concern. Many local Catholic communities rose to this moral imperative, despite tremendous financial obstacles, to fulfill their divine responsibility by providing for the moral as well as the intellectual education of the children God has entrusted to their care. In some places, progressive Catholic educational theory was benefiting youth (Bryce, 1978; Ryan, 1991).

It was Pius XI's encyclical, *The Christian Education of Youth* (1929), that explicated how the vocation of the Catholic educator is steeped in "a pure and holy love" of youth. These educators love children, the pontiff wrote, because they possess an *a priori* love of God and the Church and "have sincerely at heart the true good of family and country" (p. 48). Thus, by the early 20th century, the vocation of the Catholic educator was understood to be a tangible expression of the theological virtue of charity. Catholic educators were those members of the Catholic community who responded generously to God's call by devoting their minds and hearts, oftentimes at great personal sacrifice, to provide youth an authentic formation.

Pius XII (1958, 1979) built upon this patrimony, writing that it is the incarnation of God's love which educators have for youth, conveyed through an intimate communication between souls, which best prepares students to be the architects of the social restoration of all things in Christ. School is a place for youth to prepare for their public life and work, the Pope wrote, for it will be in their temporal careers that men and women will realize their highest spiritual destiny as members of God's kingdom.

For contemporary Catholic educators, these documents synthesize the Church's teaching of the late 19th and early 20th centuries, particularly as it concerns their vocation. Not only did the Church remind educators that they are not merely instructors or good classroom and school managers; more importantly, they are called by God to engage their students in a program of moral formation, one that inculcates the knowledge, skills, and values they will need to function in their role as the architects of the social restoration of all things in Christ.

While some have criticized the Church's stance toward the world during this era as antimodern, this stance might also be characterized as justly critical of those false ideologies that threaten authentic human freedom and which, over the course of the decades, have proven themselves to enslave men and women. It was the Church's stance against modern educational theories, as this stance was articulated in these documents of the late 19th and early 20th centuries, that prophesied accurately the deleterious effects modern educational programs would have upon the decision-making capacity of youth once they became the next generation's adults.

It is this decidedly critical vision of modern society that Vatican II seized upon as the Council described the role of the Church in the modern world. This critical vision serves in the post-Vatican II era as the foundation for understanding what educational excellence involves on the part of the men and women who have devoted their lives to forming youth.

Visions of Excellence: Theological Perspectives from the Post-Vatican II Church (1960- 1990)

> **The educator's vocation is one of many gifts God has given to the Church.**
> • Cite particular instances where teachers and administrators in your school have likened their work to a ministry.
> • Envision how educators in your school might express more concretely that their work is a ministry.
> • Can you relate each Beatitude to a particular teacher or administrator in your school?
> • How might their Christian heroism be celebrated within your school community?

Theologians and historians have oftentimes seized upon Pope John XXIII's call for *aggiornamento* to characterize the 1960s as the dawn of a new era marking the Church's openness to the modern world (Dulles, 1988, p. 10). Indeed, *The Pastoral Constitution on the Church in the Modern World (1965c, 1988, GS)* did stress this theme, particularly when the Council stated that "[a]t all times the Church carries the responsibility of reading the signs of the time and of interpreting them in the light of the Gospel, if it is to carry out its task....[that is] real social and cultural transformation whose repercussions are felt too on the religious level" (*GS*, #4).

The *Decree on the Apostolate of Lay People* (1965b, 1988, *AA*), for example, applied the theme of *aggiornamento* to the concrete situation where the Church and the world interface, the world of work, envisioning how through their work the laity can participate directly in cultural transformation. The Council declared: "The characteristic of the lay state being a life led in the midst of the world and of secular affairs, laymen are called by God to make of their apostolate, through the vigor of their Christian spirit, a leaven in the world" (*AA*, #2). The Council's challenge to the laity involved viewing their human labor not so much as a job to be completed, but more as an apostolate through which every Christian can actively participate in bringing the Church's mission toward fulfillment.

Two decades after the Council, Dulles' (1988) study of the ideals contained in its documents led him to conclude: "Statements such as these seemed to allow for a dynamic and progressive understanding of the church's teaching, accommodated to the American spirit of exploration and change" (pp. 10-11). However, as our scriptural and theological reflections concerning the vocation of the Catholic educator have indicated, Vatican II's *aggiornamento* was not quite as novel or far sweeping as Dulles' conclusion suggests. In fact, the Council's call to renewal reiterated and expanded ideals previously espoused in Church teaching, particularly its teaching about educating youth.

This is not to say, however, the Second Vatican Council accomplished little in terms of Catholic education. Quite the contrary! Vatican II built upon Church's teaching as it had been articulated during the previous two centuries. The Council also clarified more completely the vocation of the Catholic educator, particularly the role educators play in forming youth who are justly critical of the temporal order and who are willing to participate actively in its renewal.

• the Second Vatican Council...

In its *Decree on the Apostolate of Lay People* (1965b, 1988, *AA*), the Second Vatican Council turned its attention to the lay apostolate, calling men and women to a deeper awareness of their responsibility to give their lives in service to Christ and the Church (*AA*, #1). Though there are a diversity of activities that Christians can engage in to be of service, there is a unity of mission (*AA*, #2), that is, all Christians are called to evangelize and sanctify others according to the life and values of the Gospel. Christian men and women give witness not only through their family and civic sense, but also through their honest, just, sincere, and courteous dealings with others, as well as through their moral courage. Another important means of Christian witness is through the professions (*AA*, #4).

Thus, while the Sacrament of Baptism initiates individuals into the life of the Church, baptism also invites Christian men and women to participate more deeply in the Church's mission. Through their ministries, as these are expressed in the apostolate of the laity, Christians "seek [God's] will in everything, see Christ in all [people], acquaintance or stranger, make sound judgments on the true meaning and value of temporal realities both in themselves and in relation to [humanity's] end" (*AA*, #4). Through all that Christians do, and as a consequence of the spiritual sacrifices they make, Christians everywhere make the charity of Christ the soul of all their apostolate (*AA*, #3).

The vocation of the Catholic educator is one call particularly well-suited to this mission. For example, through their individual and collective witness in schools, educators "take a more active part...in the explanation and defense of Christian principles and in the correct application of them to the problems of our times" (*AA*, #6). As teachers and administrators struggle to provide for the moral and intellectual needs of youth, they also represent Christ's heroic charity as they struggle to alleviate their students' needs (*AA*, #8). Additionally, educators encourage the renewal of the temporal order as they form their students intellectually and morally, especially as they prepare them to undertake their vocation and to utilize their talents and gifts to govern the world wisely (*AA*, #14). Through their special call, teachers and administrators accept the responsibility and concomitant duty to attend to the apostolic formation of youth, particularly in its doctrinal, spiritual, and practical dimensions (*AA*, #30).

While the *Decree on the Apostolate of the Laity* situates the vocation of the Catholic educator within the general framework of all Christian vocations, the Council's *Declaration on Christian Education* (1965a, 1988, *GE*) specifies the work through which Catholic educators express their vocation. For example, this document calls for educators to prepare their students to undertake an active role in society, especially its economic and political spheres, so that when their students become Christian adults, they will have been prepared to contribute to the good of society as a whole (*GE*, Preface). Furthermore, educators need to be mindful of developing their students' intellectual capacities, of honing their ability to make sound judgments, of enabling them to delight in their cultural heritage, and learning how to incorporate and act upon a sense of values. In addition to all these important responsibilities, educators must also convey the knowledge and skills their students will need for a professional life (GE, #5).

The Second Vatican Council expressed what had become, by the 1960s, perennial themes for Catholic educators. At the same time, the Council extended this heritage by rooting the vocation of the Catholic educator within the vocation shared by all Christian laity. Thus, while all Christians are called to teach, sanctify, and govern the world, the Catholic educator's relationship with youth provides a privileged context within which teachers and administrators give personal witness to the Good News and exemplify the vocation of the laity in a most powerful way. Not only do these men and women teach youth by their words and acts; they also provide heroic witness to the requirements of Christian sanctity by encouraging their students to develop their gifts and talents so that they may govern the world wisely. Excellence in this vocation is achieved, then, not only as students learn intellectual matters but, more so, as they learn to accept their responsibilities to effect the renewal of both Church and society in the next generation.

While the vocation of the Catholic educator is a special vocation, it is also indispensable, not only for the Christian formation of youth, but also for the Catholic community itself. As the Second Vatican Council expressed this notion in its *Declaration on Christian Education*:

> Splendid, therefore, and of the highest importance is the vocation of those who help parents in carrying out their duties and act in the name of the community by undertaking a teaching career. This vocation requires special qualities of mind and heart, most careful preparation, and a constant readiness to accept new ideas and to adapt the old. (*GE*, #5)

Thus, while the educational ministry is one of many vocations God has given the Church, because of its importance in forming the next generation of Catholics, the Council urged that it be undertaken only after educators have received a specialized formation (*GE*, #8).

• the post-Vatican II era...

What is this specialized formation and of what does it consist? It is this question that the Congregation for Catholic Education answered in two documents it issued, *Lay Catholics in Schools: Witnesses to Faith* (*LLC*) and *The Religious Dimension of Education in a Catholic School* (*RDECS*).

Nearly two decades following the close of Vatican II, the Congregation for Catholic Education aggregated the Church's rich tradition pertaining to the vocation of the Catholic educator in its 1982 document, entitled *Lay Catholics in Schools: Witnesses to Faith* (1982, 1988, *LLC*). This document is perhaps the most singularly important post-conciliar document for Catholic educators, because the question it responds to is at the heart of the Catholic educator's vocation: "What is a *professional* educator in a *Catholic* sense?"

The Congregation responded to this question by reiterating much of what had been articulated in previous Church documents, namely, that the identity of the Catholic educator is discovered in the fact that the educator's work is a divine vocation, not merely one of many secular professions (*LLC*, #37). Further, the Congregation reminded educators that their work in schools is the primary means through which they express their identity as members of the Christian community. For Catholic educators, teacher and administrator professionalism is not simply what these educators do in their classrooms and schools, but rather, how they synthesize faith, culture, and life through their personal life witness (*LLC*, #25-36). The professional work that Catholic educators engage in, then, is primarily religious not secular. That is, in their classrooms and schools, Catholic educators provide a living witness to their faith in the Risen Lord.

For Catholic educators to be more capable of providing a personal life witness, *Lay Catholics in Schools* calls for the development of a formative program for educators. Setting this call within the context of a description of the formative program that Catholic educators should provide to their students, we can infer that a formative program for educators should stress experiences enabling them to:

- develop their human faculties;
- expand their professional capabilities;
- promote an ethical and social consciousness;
- be aware of God's transcendence; and,
- continue their religious education.

This formative program stands in stark contrast to most, if not all, secular approaches to faculty development and in-service programs which focus almost exclusively upon techniques, that is, *what* educators do. Instead, the Congregation's vision of formative faculty development

"Staff development" frequently connotes that educators need to develop the technical skills associated with good schooling.

- *In what specific ways does the Church's educational thought challenge this premise? What is it that Catholic educators really need to develop?*
- *Were a program of "faculty formation" to be introduced in your school, what issues does the Church suggest the faculty and administration need to consider?*
- *What structures need to be put into place if your teachers and administrators are to learn more about the vocation that is the heart of their professional practice?*

challenges teachers and administrators to engage in activities that will help them to better understand *why* they do *what* they do—to enable their students to be strong and responsible, to possess the capacity to make free and correct choices, to be open to truth, to form a clear idea about the meaning of life, to be are socially aware, and to exude a profound civic and political responsibility—making classrooms and schools places that offer youth a formative program through which educators "make human beings more human" (*LLC*, #18).

In its call for a specialized formation for Catholic educators, the Congregation for Catholic Education significantly redirected the focus of teacher and educator professionalism. Not undermining the significance of professional preparation, the Congregation reminded Catholic educators that they devote themselves to their profession for an *a priori* reason, that is, to provide a personal life witness. It is their witness that prepares students today to engage in activities that will effect the reality of God's kingdom in the next generation (*LLC*, #20).

The vocation of the Catholic educator, then, is a divine summons to evangelize youth, a call from God that constitutes a great hope for all the Church. "Very few Catholics...have the opportunity that the educator has to accomplish the very purpose of evangelization: the incarnation of the Christian message in the lives of men and women" (*LLC*, #31). Through their vocation, educators gradually bring about the integration of temporal reality with the Gospel in order that the Gospel can reach eventually into the lives of all men and women (*LLC*, #81). Without a specialized formation, one steeped in the substantive aspects of their vocation, it is difficult to see how Catholic educators will be able to provide a personal life witness in the classrooms and schools.

In 1988, the Congregation for Catholic Education completed its analysis of Catholic education in the first twenty-five years following the close of Vatican II, issuing the document entitled *The Religious Dimension of Education in a Catholic School (RDECS)*. Focusing first upon the subject of education, youth, and the tragic situation confronting them, the Congregation commented that while in "a Catholic school, as in any school, one can find young people who are outstanding in every way—in religious attitude, moral behaviour, and academic achievement" (*RDECS*, #18), the sad fact is that for

> ...some of today's youth, the years spent in a Catholic school seem to have scarcely any effect. They seem to have a negative attitude toward all the various ways in which a Christian life is expressed—prayer, participation in the Mass, or frequenting the Sacraments. Some even reject these expressions outright, especially those associated with an institutional Church. (*RDECS*, #19)

The Congregation insisted, however, that this critical attitude is symptomatic of deeper and more profound questions of a moral nature, for

The teaching of religious attitudes and behaviors is oftentimes relegated to the religion teachers or to one of the Catholic school's pastoral ministers.

- *Ideally, who are the religious educators in your school? How might this become a practical reality?*
- *Identify how moral formation could be infused throughout your school's entire educational program.*
- *What do teachers and administrators in your school need if they are to infuse moral education into all aspects of their work?*
- *How might parents become more effectively involved in and supportive of your school's religious education program?*

example, questions about the true value and ultimate meaning of life in a technologically-driven, materialistic culture.

By setting the education of youth within the context of Catholic educational philosophy (i.e., where the student is the subject of education), the Congregation identified the primary moral challenge confronting Catholic educators in the post-Vatican II era. This moral challenge is not about how educators will improve learning outcomes, but rather, how they will foster and promote the dialogue between faith and culture within every academic discipline. The primary task that Catholic school administrators, in particular, must undertake is to foster and develop an educational environment where teachers will use the curriculum as a vehicle through which students will learn to leave doubt and cynicism behind, to realize that God is actively at work in the world, and to enter the joy of His kingdom. As the Congregation described this matter, in the school

> ...God cannot be the Great Absent One or the unwelcome intruder. The Creator does not put obstacles in the path of someone trying to learn more about the universe He created, a universe which is given new significance when seen with the eyes of faith. (*RDECS*, #51)

God calls Catholic educators, then, to "respond to the questions which come from the restless and critical minds of the young" (RDECS, #23), struggling always to break through the wall of indifference and standing ready to offer youth the knowledge that embraces Christian wisdom. To foster this outcome, teachers and administrators must work together to develop a school climate that enables their students to appreciate their school's unique environment (RDECS, #26). This will be the case, the Congregation argued, only when educators are "especially concerned with the creation of a community climate permeated by the Gospel spirit of freedom and love" (RDECS, #38).

It is important to note how the Congregation for Catholic Education views the relationship involving educators, the curriculum, and students. For the Congregation, educators are not subject area experts who only communicate curriculum to students, as if the most crucial dimension of educating youth is how teachers transmit the curriculum to their students. Instead, the Congregation envisions the curriculum as the medium through which teachers communicate something of momentous consequence, the synthesis of faith, culture, and life that young men and women need. These lessons concern what is of meaning and purpose in human existence.

Without professional Catholic educators, young men and women are deprived of what true education is all about, from a Catholic perspective, that synthesis of faith, culture, and life that liberates human beings from the power of evil.

Catholic educators engage themselves and their students in "thinking about matters as a Catholic would" (Newman, 1927, 1987).

- *Describe how teachers and administrators exercise and model for their students a "critical consciousness."*
- *In light of the Church's teaching, ought the interchange of ideas between administrators, teachers, and students be characterized by uniformity? Why (not)?*
- *How might the lively interchange of critical ideas be at the heart of a school's identity?*
- *For Catholic educators, then, what really transpires in their conversations with one another, their students, and parents?*
- *Identify situations where the educator's prophetic role is expressed and understood in your school.*

The pastoral dimensions of the vocation of the Catholic educator involve forming a student's moral character.

- *Why do Church documents focus first upon the student? What might this suggest about the educator's vocation?*
- *Identify ways that parents may be invited to aid the faculty to better understand what students really need.*
- *What skills do Catholic educators need to be able to understand what their students truly need?*
- *How might this vision of the Catholic educator's vocation transform educational practice in your school?*

From this perspective, the Catholic school is a very privileged place, indeed. In it, a community of educators engages students in a formative program of an academic and moral learning. These activities, in turn, enable young men and women to grow beyond a negative attitude towards the world and human existence evident in their harsh and cynical attitude toward authority. In a Catholic school, as young men and women learn to appreciate all that is implied in the Christian vision of human existence, they will gradually realize the synthesis of faith and culture that gives ultimate meaning and purpose to their lives. And, as adults, the restlessness that could have given way to doubt and cynicism will have been healed. In its place will be an attitude informed by Christian optimism, one helping them to experience the profound peace and joy of living one's life in God's service for the promotion of His kingdom.

The questions underlying youths' restless and critical attitude frame the context for Catholic education, in general, and the vocation of the Catholic educator, in particular, for the philosophical and theological basis of Catholic education is its subject, namely, the student's growth as a human being created in God's image and likeness. Without this focus, it is easy to reduce educating youth to the cafeteria of subjects and activities that can be offered in a school's curriculum. In schools like these, students make selections based upon taste. Teachers focus upon teaching their subjects. And, administrators seek to maintain a comfortable status quo.

In contrast, the vocation of the Catholic educator suggests that true professionalism is discovered as educators love their students and give tangible expression to it through all that they do. As students experience and come to trust the love of Christ made incarnate for them in the words and actions of their teachers and administrators, they will become more engaged in and committed to their educational process (*RDECS*, #110). They will do what is necessary to achieve their true fulfillment as sons and daughters of God.

• summary: the vocation of the Catholic educator— theological reflections from the post-Vatican II Church...

This survey of Church tradition in the decades immediately following the Second Vatican Council shows us how the Church continued to clarify the issues involved in educating youth, in general, and the vocation of the Catholic educator, in particular. Grounding this particular vocation in the call of all baptized Christians to proclaim the Good News, the Council spoke of the "excellence of the teaching vocation" and its special role in promoting the renewal of the world and the Church (*DCE*, Conclusion).

Documents issued by the Congregation for Catholic Education reiterated Church tradition as it concerned educating youth, calling upon educators to give personal witness to Christ, not only through *what* they do as teachers and administrators, but more importantly, by expressing *why* they do *what* they do through all of their professional endeavors. It is through the school apostolate that young men and women will hear the Good News prophetically announced and experience the Risen Christ present in their midst (*CS*, #43). In sum, the Congregation reminded teachers and administrators that educating youth is not merely a job, but more importantly, a vocation to provide youth the secure moral and intellectual foundation that will enable them to participate in the renewal of the temporal sphere by accepting the consequences of the vocation they share as baptized Christians.

For Catholic teachers and administrators, the challenges incumbent upon them are momentous. These educators form their students to see how sin and evil are present in their lives and the world, the consequence of which leads inevitably to cynicism, despair, and nihilism. By interacting with their students, Catholic educators mediate the hope provided by their faith in the Lord Jesus. But most especially, through an intimate contact of soul with soul, achieved as Catholic teachers and administrators provide an authentic formation for their students, these educators help their students to realize that the troublesome and perplexing questions evident in their restless hearts are, in actuality, the living reminder of God's presence, their Creator calling each of them to a deeper relationship with Him.

The vocation of the Catholic educator is not simply a call to teach in a classroom or to manage a school competently. It is, in the words of the Second Vatican Council, a vocation where men and women "make of their apostolate, through the vigor of their Christian spirit, a leaven in the world" (*DAL*, #2). Educators achieve this sublime goal by using their talents in teaching and school administration to communicate God's love for youth, to prophetically announce God's challenges, to dare young men and women to utilize their God-given gifts, and to respond to God's summons in their own lives. In short, educators are those disciples who help youth to hear the Good News, to turn from sin, and to experience salvation. For these educators, true professionalism and excellence are achieved to the degree that their hearts are animated by God's love and they share it with the young men and women that parents, the Church, and civil society have entrusted to their professional and ministerial care.

Chapter 5

Very Practical Matters for Catholic Educators: The Theological Virtues and Educational Practice

Our topic is "The Vocation of the Catholic Educator." Up to this point, we have examined not only the context within which educational practice transpires, demarcating what separates good educators from their truly excellent counterparts. We have also surveyed literature from the heritage of the Catholic faith, considering both scripture and Church tradition. These efforts have enabled us to develop a theological framework for reflecting upon the vocation of those men and women God calls to serve as Catholic educators. We have unearthed norms providing insight into educational excellence, particularly as this concept might be conceived from a distinctively Catholic perspective and as it might be practiced in classrooms and schools.

Distinguishing between good and excellent schools, Sergiovanni (1995) has reminded us that we must not overlook *what* educators do. Competence in managing classrooms and schools, nurturing good working relations, and providing good curriculum and instruction are the essential building blocks comprising the solid bedrock of good educational practice. Good schools, then, are characterized by teachers and administrators who devote themselves to nurturing and sustaining professional competence. These educators are dedicated to their profession; yet, they are always "on the look out" for better ways to do what they already do so well.

One of the primary indicators of educational competence are students who achieve, like their teachers and administrators, at levels exceeding their peers in other schools, even if the students do not possess the socio-economic background or educational resources demonstrated to support student achievement (Bryk, Lee, & Holland, 1993; Coleman, Hoffer, & Kilgore, 1982; Coleman & Hoffer, 1987). Competence is indicated, too, by parents and a community that are very proud of their school. They exalt its achievements. And, they recognize and reward their teachers and administrators for their professional ethic.

Sergiovanni (1995) has also reminded us that being competent as a teacher or an administrator is an altogether different matter than being excellent. To achieve excellence, teachers and administrators must first attain competence. Then, as educators endeavor to be excellent, they inquire not only into *what* they do in their classrooms and schools. More significantly, they probe into the deeper, substantive purposes of education, inquiring *why* they do *what* they do.

In an excellent school, teachers and administrators believe in what their school exists for. They strive to embody its substantive purpose through everything they say and do. Moreover, in an excellent school, student achievement is not solely a quantitative matter, measured by the scores students receive on standardized tests. More importantly, achievement is also a qualitative matter, indicated in the degree to which students have inculcated their school's purpose. They not only value it, they also want to be characterized by it. The norms of excellence set the standard for evaluating success in these schools and, in them, teachers and administrators are not only respected for their efforts on behalf of youth. Over the years, they become revered for their ethic of care.

In excellent schools, then, educators not only instruct students, that is, building into them the knowledge, skills, and values that will enable them to have a productive life as members of society. In addition, teachers and administrators in excellent schools are mindful of the purpose that motivates them to devote their lives to educating youth. Through everything these educators endeavor to do in their classrooms and schools, they intentionally draw out of their students the fundamental purpose for which their school exists and upon which they can enact what the community believes is a truly good and meaningful life.

Excellent schools, then, are not instructional factories, minting students by imposing an ideological template upon their malleable minds. Instead, these schools are incubators of cultural purposes, institutions wherein educators challenge their students to take ownership of their school's central purpose by coming to believe in it and to act upon it. Students in excellent schools accept and meet this challenge because they trust those men and women who lead them and care for them as their teachers and administrators.

Parents know, understand, and value this intentional process; they choose to send their children to these schools, even at an additional financial burden, if necessary, because they, too, believe in and support the school's substantive purpose (Coleman, 1987a, 1987b, 1991). The Church also values these schools, for they enable their students

> ... to hear the message of hope contained in the Gospel, to base their love and service of God upon this message, to achieve a vital personal relationship with Christ, and to share the Gospel's realistic view of the human condition which recognizes the fact of evil and personal sin while affirming hope. *RCDES*, (#8)

Society also values excellent schools, for these institutions form the nation's future leaders. Society knows that the moral and intellectual lessons learned in excellent schools enable students not only to exercise the rights and responsibilities that adult citizenship will confer upon them. Excellent schools will also inculcate in students the capability to make decisions based upon the common good.

In light of the theoretical distinction Sergiovanni (1995) draws between educational competence and educational excellence, the question was raised: What, then, do *Catholic* educators need to be mindful about as they build upon the bedrock of their professional competence and strive toward the elusive goal of *Catholic* educational excellence? This question has served as the principal focus of our investigation into selected literature from the scriptures and Church tradition.

Throughout our survey, we have endeavored to understand *why* Catholic educators do *what* they do, in the belief that, were Catholic educators to become more mindful of the substantive purpose at the heart of their ministry, they could strive to make it more visible through their efforts in schools and classrooms. It was asserted that good Catholic educators will become truly excellent as "mindfulness" of their vocation becomes the principal focus of and characterizes their work.

Our literature survey considered, first, how scripture has portrayed the vocation of all Christians and, second, as the vocation of the Catholic educator has been depicted in the pre-Vatican II and post-Vatican II eras. The framework developed through our literature survey demonstrated how the scriptural mandate enjoining the Lord's disciples to go forth and teach all nations was applied to the vocation of the Catholic educator, fashioning a theological rationale that could help Catholic teachers and administrators better conceive of their "work" as a "ministry" for and on behalf of youth.

Our survey of scripture and Church tradition has also enabled us to appreciate how very important the vocation of the Catholic educator has been (and continues to be) for the family, Church, and civil communities. Catholic educators are delegated a significant parental, ecclesial, and social responsibility—that of shaping the next generation of Catholic adults, especially their moral and intellectual powers—a responsibility that cannot and should not be undertaken without a special formation. Without well-formed educators who capably provide youth an "authentic formation," it is hard to conceive of a better future for families, the Church, or the nation.

At this point into our excursus concerning the vocation of the Catholic educator, we need to consider some eminently practical matters that relate this normative framework to daily life in schools. We will focus upon the theological virtues, envisioning the kind of moral excellence that God calls teachers and administrators to enact for their students. While excellence is elusive, we know that it can be achieved. For Catholic educators, in particular, excellence is a theological challenge: to embody for students today an authentic witness to the salvific effect that faith, hope, and love offer young men and women.

• faith and mission—being mindful of God's word...

While the subject of Catholic education is the individual student and the curriculum is an authentic formation, the heart of Catholic education is the vocation of the Catholic educator. The entire enterprise depends upon the generosity of those men and women God calls in each generation to assist parents to provide not only for the intellectual development of their children, but more importantly, from a religious perspective, for their moral formation.

Catholic teachers and administrators form the visible community of disciples who have been entrusted with the responsibility for educating youth. As educators of both mind and heart, these men and women practice an intricate craft, one requiring them to be responsive to both divine grace and human nature. Through this craft, one very much akin to that of the artisan who weaves diverse strands of materials into a colorful tapestry, Catholic educators work in partnership with God, parents, and their colleagues to bring to maturity the divine image and likeness that God has breathed into each students' soul. Educators promote this educational outcome, first and foremost, as they teach by example.

In the midst of the many perplexing and oftentimes unpredictable challenges that educators confront each day, the theological virtue of faith provides divine grace, one bestowing upon Catholic educators the courage to remain confident that God has called, commissioned, sent, and empowered them to proclaim the Good News. Without the courage and confidence imparted by this theological virtue, the normal difficulties and challenges that emerge in classrooms and schools can quickly turn into nagging problems. Persistent problems develop into obstacles. These obstacles then deplete the human resources required to provide for the educational needs of youth. And, once these resources have become exasperated, the work of educating youth devolves into a job and one's educational decision-making is governed by contractual requirements. Absent is the theological purpose motivating Catholic educators, that is, the abiding courage and confidence that one's work is a vocation steeped in a covenant, wherein the partners, God and the community of educators, have pledged mutual love and fidelity.

Manifesting the courage and the confidence it takes to devote one's life to the hard work of educating youth provides evidence of hearts graced with faith. And, because these teachers and administrators possess this gift, they are mindful that the Holy Spirit is present and active in their lives. Through their words and actions, they can courageously proclaim the Good News. Excellence emerges, then, as faith enables each educator to proclaim this message.

The call to transmit values to youth requires courage on the part of the Catholic educator. Identify three examples where educators in your school have acted courageously:

A)_____

B)_____

C)_____

To fulfill their mission, Catholic educators must be confident that their efforts will be efficacious. Identify three situations where educators in your school have demonstrated great confidence:

A)_____

B)_____

C)_____

In the real world of educating youth, however, the events of daily life in schools can distract even the most highly organized professionals from being mindful of the substantive purpose for their being in classrooms and schools. In light of this, Catholic educators need to take fifteen minutes each school day to be mindful of their vocation. This period of quiet can become an oasis, a refreshing place to pause and to focus upon the substantive purpose for which they are in their classrooms and schools.

Administrators, for example, need to leave their offices and classrooms behind, not to practice "management by wandering around" (Frase & Hetzel, 1990) but to find to a place of quiet where they can put aside the practical realities distracting them from their purpose. In that place, they might read and reflect, perhaps upon a text of scripture, like one of the commissioning narratives examined earlier. But, instead of reading this text as if it presents what the Risen Lord was speaking to His disciples two millennia ago, these Catholic educators might consider the Lord Jesus directing His words to them. They might contemplate the Lord challenging them, for example, to overcome their dullness and lack of belief. They might also reflect upon how the Holy Spirit works through them to proclaim God's saving acts. And, realizing that they are graced with faith and that God dwells in them, these administrators might also utter a humble thanks to God for making all of this possible, incredible as it may seem. Allowing God's Word to direct their mindfulness, administrators might find the Lord renewing His call to go out into the real world of their schools and to represent the Risen Lord as they wander around the school community.

Teachers, too, need to take fifteen minutes each day to be mindful of their vocation. They might, for example, consider themes included in the papal speeches and encyclicals that are part of the Church's heritage.

Perusing this rich body of literature, teachers might be moved by the awesome experience of realizing that God has specially called them to be His disciples and that He is present in and working through them to effect this generation's moral and intellectual renewal. Teachers might also contemplate, for example, how it is that they are servants not only of the Gospel but of parents, the Church, and society, as well. Teachers might consider how they need to be mindful about communicating more effectively the Church's message to their students so that, one day when they have their own children, the next generation of Catholic parents will realize the message underlying their teachers' lessons and be able to provide for the moral and intellectual formation of their own children. These teachers might also be mindful of how God has called and enabled them to overcome the effects of sin in their own lives so that, filled with the wisdom that is won through the grace of conversion, they are able to speak with their students about virtuous

"Mindfulness" is a metaphor describing the act of reflecting-on-practice that can enable Catholic educators to gain a theological perspective about their lives, their work, and their world.

- *As a Catholic educator, how might you respond to God's call to nurture and nourish yourself spiritually for your mission?*
- *In your daily and weekly schedule, is there a block of time you can take for yourself, to be alone, to reflect upon your vocation, and the events confronting you?*
- *How might your diocesan schools office organize a significant amount of time each year (perhaps during the summer) to reflect upon your vocation, your growth and development, and to develop plans to become a more authentic Catholic educator?*
- *When and how might all educators in your school take time to pray and reflect upon their common vocation?*

living and what this implies, especially as the trials of adolescence besiege them. Finally, these teachers might also be mindful of the power of evil at work in the world today and be moved by God to strike at its roots. Inspired by these ideals, these teachers might share with their students how they may not only be critical of sin but also how they may also utilize their God-given talents and spend their lives in the service of promoting Catholic social teaching.

As a community, too, Catholic educators might consider gathering daily to become ever more mindful of their common vocation. The community of Catholic educators might gather, for example, just prior to the beginning of each day to share a brief passage of scripture or a selection from Church tradition. Each teacher and administrator, throughout the course of the school year, might offer a short reflection upon the reading, applying it to daily challenges they are called to meet. This short service might close as members of the faculty offer intercessory prayers, naming specific individuals and their needs.

The community of Catholic educators might also consider closing each school day with a prayer service designed along similar lines. In this context, however, teachers and administrators might be assigned (or select) a short passage from scripture, read it over the intercom, and then offer a short reflection for all of the community, educators and students alike. The reflection might close with a reading of intercessions that teachers, administrators, and students have written in a book specially designated for this purpose and placed in a prominent place in the school's lobby or chapel foyer.

Daily efforts to be more mindful of the vocation of the Catholic educator are a very important dimension of Catholic educational practice. These activities focus teachers and administrators upon the purpose that has motivated them to devote their lives to forming youth. But, just as daily activities are important to remain mindful about why educators do what they do, so too are monthly and annual efforts.

Twice each semester, or perhaps even monthly, school might be canceled and a formative in-service might be held for teachers and administrators to gather for a day of reflection and spiritual renewal. Whether the day follows a formal or an informal schedule is immaterial, but it should be punctuated by the celebration of the Eucharist, presided over by the students' pastors who also bear a moral obligation concerning the education of the youth in their parishes. A more formal approach might take the form of a quarterly (or monthly) retreat that, over the course of the year, reflects upon and provides practical guidance about a particular aspect of the Catholic educator's vocation. A less formal approach might be shaped according to the group's interests, responding to current interests and issues, but always focusing upon their vocation. Annually, perhaps before the school year begins, the entire staff might go on retreat for a few days to focus on their mission. The aim of this retreat is simple: to rekindle their faith so that Catholic educators might be more confident and courageous in their ministry.

Daily, monthly, and annual prayer experiences, wherein Catholic educators take time to meet the Risen Lord and become renewed in His Spirit, should enable them to be more mindful of their vocation and to embody it in all of the busy activities that must be accomplished. Animated by the Holy Spirit, Catholic educators can then stand in the midst of the school community not only as professionals, but also as symbols of God's love expressed most perfectly in the Risen Lord. It is mindfulness of their commission to herald the culture of faith that upholds the Risen Lord as its Way, Truth, and Life that makes it possible for Catholic educators not only nurture their faith but also to become more courageous and confident as they minister to what youth truly need.

Any momentary pause, whether it is at the beginning, end, or even, during the school day itself, will enable teachers and administrators to be mindful of the substantive purpose for which they have come together. Simple events, like a daily prayer service or a quarterly retreat, can become a powerful reminder for all members of the school community about why Catholic educators do what they do. Focusing upon prayer is also a powerful symbol, communicating to students what it is they, too, are called to be. Likewise, quarterly, semi-annual, or annual events that bring the community of educators together to focus on the substantive purpose at the heart of their educational ministry reminds them about what they are called to be for one another and their students.

Educational excellence is achieved, then, as educators are mindful of and effectively communicate their school's purpose. What must not be forgotten is that the theological virtue of faith is what provides the courage and confidence that excellent Catholic educators need to remain committed to and to fulfill the demands of their ministry. Only disciples who are full of faith are able to proclaim in very practical ways the Good News to young men and women.

For the majority of young men and women, it is truly unfortunate that educators can be consciously mindful of their vocation and act upon it only in a religious school. It is also unfortunate that only in a religious school can teachers and administrators form a community of faith, one consciously seeking to symbolize for youth the synthesis of faith and culture that has meant so much to people throughout the centuries. We can only hope that every student will have the opportunity to experience the type of educational excellence that is achieved as teachers and administrators fulfill the purpose for which God has called them to serve as educators, namely, to herald the Christian faith to youth.

• hope and idealism—the word is made flesh...

Being mindful of scripture and tradition is an important first step by which Catholic educators can become more open to God's living presence and more responsive to the challenges posed by their vocation. By devoting some time each school day and each academic year to being present to God, Catholic educators can invite Him to become an animating force in their lives and work, allowing God to shape not only what they see transpiring within the confines of their classrooms and schools but also their response to it. Mindful of their purpose, Catholic educators can immerse themselves in the real world of schooling and provide a more authentic formation for their students.

In a world where evil continues to manifest its deleterious effects each day, it is difficult for many people to be confident that God continues to effect His saving purpose in the world. Today, tragedy seemingly breeds and compounds more tragedy, making even the most noble of efforts to stem the ruinous tide of social decay appear impotent. It is easy for anyone, especially educators who see these effects becoming more pronounced in the lives of their students, to experience frustration and despair and, ultimately, to conclude that something has gone so terribly awry that nothing can be done to recover humanity's lost innocence. Ultimately, fear dislodges hope as people cast about, searching in vain for new gods to calm the rising tides of despair.

When despair becomes pervasive, it is especially easy for educators to forsake courage, to adopt a cynical attitude, to look upon their work as providing merely for the intellectual formation of youth, and to neglect the more difficult task of attending to their moral formation. While this rationalization may offer some educators a convenient means to evade one's moral responsibility, Catholic educators see in the despair confronting youth the Risen Lord challenging them, just as He challenged the Eleven, to turn from their disbelief (Mark 16:14). When Catholic educators are mindful of their vocation, the Lord empowers them with courage to overcome any threat to their belief and provides them with the confidence they need to proclaim God's Word. Without this witness, educators must recall, youth will gradually lose their natural resistance to the most deadly epidemic menacing them today, what Medved (1996) calls "the plague of pessimism" infecting tens of millions of young Americans.

In its documents, the Congregation for Catholic Education has reminded Catholic educators that the daily reality they confront in their classrooms and schools is their students. These are the young men and women who are experiencing the twin realities of restlessness and temptation, not only as these are evident in human ignorance but also, and perhaps more importantly, as they become pronounced in the attitude of pessimism that makes sinfulness appear as a sensible alternative to virtuous living. Catholic educators who are mindful of their vocation

List three challenges confronting your students that you believe could lead them to despair:

A)_____

B)_____

C)_____

not only realize that the vestiges of sin are evident in their own lives, but mindfulness also graces them to rise above the false allure of sin. Ultimately, it is their conversion from sin that makes it possible for Catholic educators to assist their students to examine the presence of sin in their lives, to lead them toward healing and away from pessimism.

Neither educators nor their students need to be pessimistic or, worse yet, to despair. Though the world may have embraced the "culture of death" (John Paul II, 1995), teachers and administrators can use their words and actions to remind (and sometimes to urge) the school community to convert to the Good News and to experience salvation. In their classrooms and schools, then, it is faith that enables Catholic educators to represent the Risen Lord and to confront the pessimism which leads their students to despair and, ultimately, to death. Catholic educators stand before their students as signs of contradiction, prophetically challenging the behaviors and attitudes that are steeped in pessimism. In short, Catholic teachers and administrators herald the gospel of hope in a place where despair might be given free reign.

In very practical terms, the theological virtue of hope demands that administrators be willing to confront the ruinous tide of pessimism afflicting students today. Principals, for example, might respond by redirecting the primary focus of administrative and staff meetings, broadening the agenda to emphasize the school's primary interest, the formation of youth, and to de-emphasize routine business and administrative matters. Rather than worrying about and spending inordinate amounts of time puzzling over schedules, detention, course offerings, and supervising instruction, principals might begin each administrative meeting with a pastoral reflection, leading their colleagues to consider pessimism as it confronts youth today. The administrative staff might then engage in lively conversation about what they and their colleagues might be able to do to get at the roots of this issue and to help their students. Rather than inquiring into what bureaucratic policies and rules mandate, these educators might read a selection from scripture to inquire what God is asking of them. And, armed with a consensus about what ought to be done in their students' best interests, principals might engage in their work, looking at it being more of a pastoral ministry than a managerial endeavor.

In light of the need to challenge the pessimism that confronts youth, faculty meetings should be refocused so that the faculty will be given multiple opportunities to consider their vocation and its challenges concerning the practical issues they must deal with in their classrooms. Rather than attending solely to professional and administrative matters that are just as easily communicated through memoranda, faculty meetings could focus primarily upon the subject of education, that is, the students. The faculty, for example, might report, discuss, and document the signs of pessimism emerging in their classrooms, in the corridors,

The vocation of the Catholic educator is be a witness to evangelical hope.

- *Reflect upon an instance where a student has related a personal struggle with hopelessness and despair.*
- *What was absent in the student's life?*
- *In what concrete ways could your colleagues on the faculty and administration help you to better serve this student?*
- *Cite concrete ways that your school can exercise its pastoral obligations by providing opportunities for all members of the school community to confront issues of hopelessness.*

in after-school activities, or even as they perceive pessimism present in their students' homes. The faculty might examine the facts they gather, searching for the root causes of these attitudes and behaviors. Mindful of their vocation, the faculty might prayerfully direct its attention to what God is asking them to do to help their students deal more effectively with evil as it intrudes into school life.

Concretely, at a faculty meeting that focuses primarily upon the subject of education, Catholic educators might wonder aloud, for example, about how skepticism concerning religion and indifference to its practice might evidence the subtle, yet powerful influences of evil encroaching upon their students' lives. Perhaps this discussion might provoke some educators to become more mindful of their own attitudes concerning religious practices in their classrooms and school. They might consider attending religious exercises with greater enthusiasm, making classroom prayer more personal, praising virtuous behavior, and modeling more effectively the norms of Christian decency. Perhaps, too, this discussion might challenge other educators to deepen their faith and hope, and in doing so, to contribute more fully to the school's program of moral formation, remembering that their work in a school is, primarily, a ministry God has entrusted to them.

Skepticism, indifferentism, and laxity about the place of religion in human existence leads inevitably to a gradual decline in moral standards, and for Catholic educators, what excellent schools stand both for and against. There is no choice for Catholic educators in the matter of confronting evil. As history has evidenced so clearly, when teachers leave sinful behaviors and attitudes unchallenged, the powerful influences of evil lead their students inevitably to judge that God is irrelevant to the important matters of human existence. Evil, then, compounds upon evil, with its deleterious effects visiting the next generation, with far greater consequences.

While it is difficult for anyone to confront behaviors that contradict the Gospel, Catholic educators know, too, that when youth are left unchallenged, they ultimately will become practical atheists, that is, people possessing little or no hope in God's saving power. Where pessimism and despair reign, death evolves as the concluding chapter to a depraved life where a human being has successfully evaded the power of God's hope. Some educators might believe that confronting their students' misbehavior is trivial and unrelated to educating youth, a matter better left to parents; but, for Catholic educators, student behavior and the attitudes they exhibit are at the heart of the formative process. For these teachers and administrators, hope is normative, setting the standard against which all people can discern right from wrong, the important from the superfluous, and the necessary from the transitory.

Catholic educators, then, minister to the moral and intellectual formation of youth by upholding these ideals, first, as they exemplify it in their own lives and, second, in the many ways they challenge evil in their own lives, in the lives of their students, and in their community as well. It is antithetical to the vocation of the Catholic educator for teachers and administrators to neglect their obligation to proclaim the Good News by saying "kids will be kids" or "forget it, it's not anything new, they'll get over it just like we did." Eventually, this benign neglect allows evil to establish a foothold within the school community. Ultimately, the power of evil will erode the school's substantive purpose.

Hope, borne of the Christian gospel, challenges Catholic educators to leave their reflective moments behind, to re-enter the real world of their school, and to engender the theological virtue of hope through all they do. In their classrooms and schools, mindfulness enables Catholic educators to proclaim this virtue, to break through their students' hardness of heart, to get beyond their grumbling, and to be effective ministers of God's saving grace. These educators herald the Good News that God continues to call young people to perfect their lives, to go forward into the world, and to effect the social reconstruction of all things in Christ. With the courage and confidence provided by faith in the Risen Lord, there is no need for anyone to despair.

Without the idealism spurred by the theological virtue of hope, Catholic educators may be good teachers and administrators who provide for the intellectual needs of youth. But, having lost sight of their vocation, they will not become excellent Catholic educators, for they will have failed to provide their students the moral formation that alone enables youth to experience the optimism provided by the virtue of hope and to respond to it by devoting their lives to Christ's saving mission.

These lofty ideals, rooted in the heritage of Catholic educational theory, remind Catholic educators that excellence requires hearts full of hope, the virtue giving them the ability to interpret for their students the pessimistic "signs of the times" in the light of the Christian gospel. Likewise, excellence also connotes that Catholic educators might not be appreciated at first for their efforts on behalf of students, because these men and women stand for something in a world that would prefer teachers and administrators to stand for everything.

• charity and witness—the Word dwells among us...

Scripture and tradition are, for Catholic educators, living testimony of God's continuing presence and activity in the midst of human history. They provide a living reminder of what God promises for His people, what He has created them for, and what He calls them to be. Scripture and tradition also recall how all humanity always stands in need of God's redeeming grace.

Being mindful of this heritage and applying it to the context of life and work in schools is an important discipline for Catholic educa-

> *To serve students, Catholic educators must confront the forces of evil seeking to thwart their mission*.
> - *Identify a situation where you believed a formative issue was clear, but were required to deny this situation's formative aspects.*
> - *Cite the primary ways you experience yourself being compelled to turn your focus toward the instructional aspects of teaching and away from its formative aspects.*
> - *In what concrete ways could you go about reversing this trend, transforming your work into a ministry?*

tors, for it strengthens and nourishes in them the theological virtues of faith and hope. Mindfulness also fosters an abiding confidence in God and His continued saving actions. Furthermore, mindfulness inspires in Catholic educators a vision informed by the theological virtue of hope, not only that they can help their students to rise above their pessimism and sin, but also, through the grace of conversion, to grow in faith and hope. When Catholic educators proclaim this Good News, they engage themselves in holy work, a labor of love, something borne of a generous heart. For Catholic educators, the proclamation of the Good News is not an experience reserved to Sunday liturgy; it is God's living Word which they address each and every day to their students.

The vocation of the Catholic educator is a call to proclaim God's saving message in a privileged context, the school and its classrooms. But what does the theological virtue of love demand of those who wish to fulfill their vocation as Catholic educators? Paul's first letter to the Corinthians provides a scriptural perspective illuminating the stringent demands that the theological virtue of love imposes upon those who would wish to educate youth.

In this letter, Paul invokes the metaphor of the human body to describe the disciple's work and the care each disciple must take to build upon the sure foundation which is Jesus Christ (3:10-11). The central issue, for Paul, is that the individual members of the Christian community must understand how God has called each of them to contribute their unique gifts and to work, as one community, for the building of God's kingdom. Just as the human body has many individual parts, each expressing its excellence by contributing to the well-functioning of the human organism, so too, Paul reminds the Corinthians, the Christian community possesses many diverse gifts, each of which has been given by God to further the community's good-functioning.

The excellence of the Christian community is not discovered in the perfection of its individual members who draw attention to themselves and their achievements, setting themselves apart from other members of the community who do not possess similar gifts in abundance. Rather, the excellence of the Christian community is discovered when each of its members freely give their gifts to bring about the fulfillment of the community's purpose. Just as there is no room in this community for self-interested individualism, neither is there any room for mindless conformity. Instead, excellence is achieved as unique individuals accept their rights and exercise their concomitant responsibilities as members of the Christian community, what Paul calls "freedom under grace."

As Paul reminded the Corinthian community, he also reminds Catholic educators that, without the good functioning of each part, the whole itself is deficient (1 Corinthians 12:12-26). What makes the whole enterprise of the educational community function well, is not how

Some identify a "Catholic" school with religion classes and religious symbols and practices.
- *What do scripture and Church tradition suggest identifies a Catholic school?*
- *What does Paul suggest that transpires in the conversations and relationships between Catholic educators and their students?*
- *In what ways do the conversations educators have with their students communicate most effectively the school's Catholic identity?*
- *How might these matters be "the heart" of the vocation of the Catholic educator?*

each teacher or administrator excels, but how the love of God and neighbor motivates each member of the school community to contribute to the good functioning of the whole educational enterprise.

For Paul, the mystery that makes it possible for human beings to sacrifice their self-interest for the common good is love. He wrote to the Corinthians:

> Love is patient; love is kind and envies no one. Love is never boastful, nor conceited, nor rude; never selfish, not quick to take offence. Love knows no score of wrongs; does not gloat over other men's sins, but delights in the truth. There is nothing love cannot face; there is no limit to its faith, its hope, and its endurance. (1 Corinthians 12:4-7, NEB)

For Catholic educators, the real world of their classrooms and schools is the crucible wherein their excellence is put to the test. In all that they say and do, Catholic educators manifest their excellence when they are patient, not only with themselves and one another, but with their students too. Excellence is manifested when Catholic educators are kind, when they are not envious, and when they live in the humble awareness that God has given each of them many gifts to bring to fulfillment their school's purpose. Excellence is revealed as Catholic educators encourage one another and their students to bring to perfection all that God has entrusted to them. Finally, excellence appears when teachers and principals remind their students that the perfection of their gifts is not for selfish purposes, but what brings their school community (and one day, the world) to perfection.

Excellence is manifest further by the words and actions of Catholic educators who do not boast about themselves and their accomplishments; neither are these men and women conceited nor are they rude. Instead, in all that they do, excellence becomes apparent in the fact that Catholic educators give thanks to God for their achievements, for they know that their success has been made possible only through God's grace.

Even more remarkably, excellence is manifest as Catholic educators overcome the hurts they experience, that is, Catholic educators forgive one another and their students, as God has forgiven them. And, as a consequence, they are able to take delight in one another, to enjoy their presence in the school, and together, to accept the call God has given to them to "Go forth to every part of the world, and proclaim the Good News to the whole creation" (Mark 15:15).

Without love, it is impossible for any human being to allow the common good to transcend one's calculative self-interest. Without love, it is impossible for human beings to submit themselves to another's demands or to forgive them for their wrong-doings. Mindful of God's love, Catholic educators realize that their words and actions are God's

The virtue of charity is the foundation of all Christian ministry.
- *Identify ways to make your school and its classrooms places that communicate God's love.*
- *How might faculty evaluation become a moment for administrators and teachers to identify and recognize the gifts that God has given to the school?*
- *Design a service for celebrating how members of the school community have healed the wounds of sin and division and have become reconciled.*

words and actions, calling all members of the school community to love one another as God has loved them. As they are able to bring this vision of excellence to fulfillment, the school and its classrooms are the place where God dwells. Its perfection is found in the perfection of its members.

It is the power of God's love that enables men and women to sacrifice their lives and to engage in the formation of those youth who will serve Christ, the Church, and society in building God's kingdom during the next generation. While faith and hope inspire Catholic educators to forsake rest and comfort so that youth might receive an authentic formation, it is charity, the very love of God Himself, that empowers Catholic educators to toil amidst all of the weariness and discomfort associated with educating youth. Pius XII (1945, 1979) was most eloquent in proclaiming this ideal when he contrasted Catholic educators with their secular peers:

> [T]here are other men and women inflamed with a holier ideal and anxious to perform their duty in conformity with the principles of the Gospel. These feel themselves irresistibly drawn to protect children from evil in order to give them to God, to undergo weariness and discomfort in order to form people who will service Christ, the Church and human society in a worthy manner. And this is your ideal; this is the love that has conquered your hearts and to which you have pledged your lives!
>
> It is this splendid ideal, this love which participates of the love of God Himself, which inspires you and sweetens the severity of your work. (p. 342)

Only the power of God's love can conquer the tides of evil, the pessimism buffeting youth, and heal the chaos and ruins that lie ravaged in its devastating wake.

• Summary: Theological Mindfulness—Authentic Educational Practice that Liberates...

As I write about the relationship of mindfulness, the theological virtues, and the vocation of the Catholic educator, I recall a teacher in a diocesan high school where I have led several in-service programs. Even though I only met this woman once (or maybe twice), I do know that she was respected not only for her work (she was a very good teacher) but, more especially, for the way she modeled for the entire school what it truly means to be a Catholic educator.

Each day, year in and year out, when she would finish her lunch, this devoted educator would leave the noise of the cafeteria and the chatter of her colleagues behind and proceed in a very quiet and unobtrusive way to the school's chapel. There, each day of the week, each week of the year, for the nearly twenty years she taught at this school, she would take twenty minutes to pray the rosary. Then, when she completed her prayer (what some of her colleagues called "her routine"), she would leave the quiet of the chapel and go to her classroom to teach her afternoon classes. Without doubt, she always entered her classroom mindful of her purpose. And in those very privileged confines, her actions taught her students as eloquently as did her words.

Each day as she would pray the rosary, it was not infrequently that teachers, administrators, and students would amble by the chapel and take a peek through the glass to see if she was there. Spotting her praying the rosary, they would go on their way, feeling confident that things were okay. Sometimes, the chaplain told me, teachers and administrators would joke about who it was that this woman was praying for and who it was that she ought to be praying for. She was an excellent Catholic educator whom everyone revered and, I suspect, hoped was praying for them.

One day, while praying the rosary as was her well-established and very predictable routine, this marvelous Catholic educator collapsed and died suddenly, without having completed her rosary. Amid the shock and grief of seeing her being whisked away by an ambulance, some teachers and students began to express their grief, pain, and anguish by going to the school's chapel to pray the rosary. There, they noticed, someone had placed her rosary on the prie-dieu where she had prayed each day for all of those years. The next day, someone placed a bouquet of flowers beside her rosary.

This woman's steadfast witness of faith, hope, and love in the Risen Lord transformed her professional competence into theological excellence, a ministry through which she taught her subjects (i.e., her students as well as her colleagues) the Catholic vision of human existence in a very practical, yet powerful way. She didn't seek her own glory but, by contributing her gifts to the fulfillment of the school's purpose, she stood in its midst as a most powerful witness. She was an excellent Catholic educator, a disciple whose professional practice embodied in very personal virtues of faith, hope, and love.

Her words and actions teach us that the Catholic educator's work is a sacred trust, not simply a job. It is also a ministry, a sacrifice that generous men and women willingly make of their lives for the betterment of families, the Church, and society. It is a ministry that cannot be undertaken without careful preparation for, as ministers of the Good News, Catholic educators are disciples of Christ whose professional practice and personal witness heralds to youth in this generation God's power to renew all things through the power of His love.

When Catholic educators are mindful of their vocation, as this woman was, discipleship is not something reserved for a chosen few in times past. Discipleship is, in this age and for the children God entrusts to His disciples, a ministry which they enact each and every day, not only through what they say but, more importantly, through the testimony of their actions.

As always, however, God's invitation is a freely given gift, and in this case, one offered to youth through the generosity of the Catholic educator. It always remains up to each and every student to accept and to respond to this divine initiative, choosing to listen openheartedly or to remain steadfast and hard-hearted to those teachers and administrators who offer them the gift of the theological virtues. Excellent Catholic educators know that faith, hope, and love will liberate their students from pessimism and sin, restoring them to their proper dignity as God's beloved sons and daughters.

Chapter 6

The Vocation of the Catholic Educator: Mindfulness in Teaching and Administering

As we have seen, the vocation of the Catholic educator presents men and women with challenges that are not only professional but, more importantly, personal.

For the most part, educators are familiar with the former, their professional challenges, which require that educators not only amass an amazing array of skills but also that educators capably exercise them (Kagan, 1992). While it may be true "first learned is best learned" and that many educators do unintentionally mime those who were their first teachers, these are not professional educators who devote themselves to the very hard work of learning to teach (Carter, 1990).

At first glance, professional expertise appears to be an effortless endeavor, much akin to that of the accomplished athlete who routinely achieves what would be an amazing fete for the average human being. We know, however, that professional expertise isn't effortless. It requires practice, patience, and persistence for an individual to engage in the continuous improvement that is the hallmark of a true professional. For aspiring educators, training programs at colleges and universities ideally provide knowledge and practice in the skills of the profession. But, whatever training educators receive prior to entering their classrooms and schools for the first time, we know that it will be only as they exercise and refine their skills over the first five years of their careers that educators will hone real competence (Kagan, 1992). Over time, their competence will develop into expertise as they are mindful about what good teaching requires of them and continuously seek apply these lessons to their professional practice.

When I visit schools and am introduced to respected educators, I ask them, "What subject do you teach?" And, it is not at all unusual for them to respond, "I teach math" (or whatever the particular course or grade levels is) or "I'm the principal" (or whatever administrative role in the institutional hierarchy the individual currently occupies). Then, I ask a follow-up question, "What do you do?" For a fleeting moment, these men and women stare straight at me, perhaps wondering whether or not I am serious. Or, perhaps they are wondering about what answer

I am fishing for. But, as I look squarely into their eyes, these respected educators relate, in rather elaborate detail, the intricate subtleties involved in their work.

For example, they have told me about how they "keep an eye" on everything that goes on in their classrooms, how they are able to infer when something is awry, and how they maintain in their classrooms an atmosphere conducive to instruction and learning. Your can bet on it: there is nothing that is happenstance occurring in these classrooms.

These respected educators have also related some of the new cultural influences they perceive to be influencing youth. Homes are not necessarily the nurturing places for youth that many would hope their homes would be. Streets seem more hospitable for acts of violence than they are for games of hop-scotch, double-dutch jump rope, or stickball. Television isn't a distraction; it is a way of life making it appear that human beings can engage in the most dastardly of behaviors, without any consequences whatsoever. And so, youth tempt Fate and pay the price.

I have also been told that it is challenging enough for educators to attempt to provide good instruction to youth when they are dealing with a homogeneous population. But, today's heterogeneous student population requires new skills. The professional demands placed upon educators have expanded, they have said, not cumulatively but geometrically. All of this has made the task of educating youth a far more puzzling and complex endeavor, perhaps more daunting than it has ever been. Educating youth requires much, even of a well-seasoned veteran.

These men and women deserve respect and encouragement for devoting themselves to this very challenging profession. Against very great odds, these experts provide for youth what mere mortals might be led to conclude is virtually impossible. Through it all, however, they are mindful of their professional responsibilities and, as Sergiovanni (1995) reminds us, their managerial, interpersonal, and technical skills coalesce in such a way that competence is their trademark. Being mindful of what professional practice requires makes it possible for them to accomplish what they set about doing.

Who isn't impressed by what these educators do? Parents want their children in these classrooms. Principals wish all of their faculty could be like these accomplished educators. Their peers hold them in awe. When we see the remarkable ease with which these experts do what they do (and do so well), wouldn't it be nice if we could compile a book of recipes providing their solutions to the problems of professional practice and simply order aspiring educators to follow these recipes? Unfortunately, however, we know that following a recipe does not make a chef. Neither does blindly imitating a respected educator guarantee that one will be a respected educator. A base of fundamental competence, mindfulness of one's professional responsibilities, purposeful practice, and reflection upon practice are necessary.

In my conversations with respected educators, they have also told me, somewhat on the sly, that they sometimes have to improvise as they struggle to meet their students' educational needs. And, I have wondered, "Where do educators turn when they have to improvise?"

As familiar as researchers are with the many professional challenges incumbent upon educators, researchers are not quite as familiar with the personal challenges they confront in their professional practice. Sergiovanni (1995) points us in a promising direction with his suggestion that excellence builds upon fundamental competence. We know, for example, that teachers and administrators stand before their students as symbols of what society deems important. When educators fulfill their symbolic role, we also know that cultural values are communicated in very powerful ways, influencing and shaping how youth view their lives, their work, and their world. In short, these experts cultivate and develop not only intellectual capital, but also moral and social capital in their students (Coleman, 1987a, 1987b, 1988). More research is necessary, however, if we are to understand the personal challenges incumbent upon educators as well as we understand their professional challenges.

I must confess, however, that when highly respected, expert educators tell me all of what they do in their classrooms and schools, I become somewhat disquieted. The elaborate details relating what they do strikes me as rather hollow, in much the same way that I'd find myself disquieted if a pastor was to describe what he does in terms of the number of masses, baptisms, and funerals he performs. Or, if parents were to describe being a mother or father in terms of what they have given their children over the years. My point is: *what* educators do, as important as that is (and we must never underestimate its importance), is meaningless unless it communicates something more important—the *why* that motivated these wonderful and generous human beings to do what they do in the first place.

This all too prevalent, functionalist response, even on the part of our most respected educators, has been the implicit focus of this monograph, *The Vocation of the Catholic Educator*. Weber (1930, 1992) argued early in this century that, when the ethos shaping how people view their work places value solely upon what they do as a means to a different end, human beings unwittingly imprison themselves within an "iron cage." For Weber, this powerful metaphor encapsulated the maze of hierarchically defined rules and expectations which exert the power to reduce one's vocation to a job, one's substantive purpose to a functional role, and the freedom to make decisions about what ought to be done to calculative, rational planning so that humans can sustain and increase their capital.

When educators become imprisoned within this iron cage, the heart and soul of educating youth erodes and eventually is corrupted, that is, the substantive purpose that originally inspired people to offer their lives in the service of youth is superseded by the requirements of their functional role. They define their work contractually and, as teachers and administrators experience themselves caring about their students and what they truly need, the terms of the educators' contracts suddenly intervene and encumber their decision-making process, rendering them incapable of expressing their heartfelt and personal care.

The functional view of teaching and administering in schools so permeates modern consciousness that what educators do in their schools and classrooms has become a more important focus than the substantive reason, the why, at the heart of their work. Many educators know this sad fact, all too well. For them, school is a place where they work, but it is not a place where they engage in the intimate conversations with their students and colleagues about their identity and mission as people of God, as Pius XII (1955) reminds us schools and classrooms should be. The focus of all their preparation is upon all the knowledge and skills they must convey to their students, not upon the subject they teach, the student, whose mind and heart are the principal focus for Catholic educators. In those schools where the substantive purpose for educating youth is absent, principals are preoccupied with organizational problems, worrying more about routine maintenance and how to comply with district, states and federal mandates than they are worried about formative faculty development and meeting their students' true needs. Sadly, some educators hope just to be able to make it through the day without an incident occurring.

Perhaps some readers might be experiencing discomfort and want to object to this caricature I have drawn, arguing that it portrays an extremist, either-or, take it or leave it worldview that does not represent the classrooms and schools they know. And, I am sure that for many readers the caricature doesn't. But, to the degree that this caricature accurately portrays teachers and administrators who focus solely upon what they do in order to fulfill their professional role expectations, the caricature serves as a healthy reminder that the failure to be mindful of the personal demands incumbent upon teachers and administrators will ultimately manifest itself in a form of heartless professionalism that places calculative self-interest before the true interests of youth. In contrast, mindfulness about why educators do what they do is the antidote to that form of professionalism devoid of personalism which mindlessly allows classrooms and schools to be turned into instructional factories and sweatshops.

Our survey of scripture and Church tradition has offered an alternative to this depressing and pessimistic caricature. When Catholic educators are asked what they do, these educators should be the men and women whose mindful response reflects a pervading appreciation for why they do what they do. For example, they should respond not only that they teach courses, but more importantly, the subject they really teach and care about is the individual student. These educators should also respond that they fill important roles, but are mindful that what they truly "ad-minister" (i.e., minister to) are human beings, men and women and young boys and girls, created in the image and likeness of God but still needing an authentic formation that will enable them to be disciples of God's kingdom. These educators talk about their job all right, but describe it in terms of Christian discipleship. They communicate a sense of purpose and mission that finds its inspiration in the texts of scripture and Church tradition as well as in the lives of those courageous men and women who have preceded them in Christian history, particularly those Catholic educators, in a previous generation, who served as their mentors.

Pointing out differences between those educators who focus primarily upon what they do and those who are mindful about why they do what they do is not intended to belittle or demean anyone who has responded generously to God's invitation to minister as a Catholic educator. What these reflections are intended to do is to stimulate Catholic educators to become ever more mindful about *why* they do *what* they do, in order that they might inspired to fulfill more perfectly the personal requirements of their vocation.

When Catholic educators refocus how they conceive what they do, that is, as they focus more intently upon the substantive purpose at the heart of their work in classrooms and schools, the ideological iron cage constraining them from enacting their personal responsibilities can be broken. Knowing and understanding the patrimony of Catholic educational thought, as it has been preserved in scripture and tradition, will enable Catholic educators to move beyond what can become an ethos of heartless professionalism manifesting itself in bureaucratic rules that shackle educators, making it impossible for them to express their heartfelt and personal care for youth and to provide for their true needs. Freed from the structural manacles of this functionalist ideology, Catholic educators can lead their classrooms and schools "as full partners in the church's mission of educating the whole person and of transmitting the good news of salvation in Jesus Christ to successive generations of young Americans" (John Paul II, 1987, p. 280).

For Catholic educators, it is the heritage of the Judaeo-Christian culture as it has been lived out by Catholic men and women in each generation that is the primary referent for all educational decision-making. When Catholic educators are mindful of this heritage as they go about deciding what they must do, they can consciously infuse all that they do with the more substantive theological purpose for which they engage in educating youth, namely, to provide them an authentic formation for their lives as Jesus' disciples. It is when all of the tangible aspects of educating youth reflect its substantive dimensions that we can begin to appreciate what educational excellence, for a *Catholic* educator, is truly about. As John Paul II remarked to Catholic educators during his 1987 pastoral trip to the United States, "For a Catholic educator, the church should not be looked upon merely as an employer. The church is the body of Christ, carrying on the mission of the Redeemer, through history. It is our privilege to share in that mission, to which we are called by the grace of God and in which we are engaged together" (1987, p. 280).

The vocation of the Catholic educator, then, is not only a summons to professionalism. It is also a summons to personalism, challenging Catholic teachers and administrators to proclaim the Church's heritage through the example of their lives. Their words and actions express the theological virtues of faith, hope, and love in the name and place of those parents who have entrusted their children to their care.

Ultimately, it is when the Catholic educator's vocation, the *why*, is heralded through one's words and actions, the *what*, that students become more mindful that it is the Risen Lord teaching in their midst. Some students might not realize Who it is that is teaching them. Many students will not believe His message as it is expressed by their teachers and administrators. And, some students will reject His message outright. But, it is these excellent teachers and administrators who provide opportunities for their students to encounter the Risen Lord calling them to "go forth and teach all nations" (Mark 16:15). This substantive purpose, when it is translated into pedagogical and administrative practice, is the "glue" binding together and perfecting what is done in schools.

When this substantive purpose is absent from educational decision-making, an ominous iron cage descends upon teachers and administrators as teacher-proofed curricula are mindlessly enacted by men and women whose professional practice is governed by educational cookbooks and contractual obligations. God's covenant with His people is judged irrelevant to, if not dismissed outright from their educational decision-making. Then, what is wrong is judged to be right and the next generation, having found no heroic role models in their teachers and principals, loses its moral compass. As our survey of the Church's tradition has indicated, this scenario is not pessimistic; indeed, it reflects quite accurately the guiding ethic in educational practice during the late-19th century. It was this scenario Pius IX (1864, 1979) prophetically decried.

Without heroic educators who are willing to sacrifice themselves in order to help youth to see that there are true values, that there is hope where perhaps they only experience fear, that standing firm against a culture that wants everything is virtuous, we can be sure that the future will be bleak.

All is not lost, however. Pessimism and despair do not reign. The Risen Lord has broken the bonds of death. The vocation of the Catholic educator offers great hope to parents, the Church, and society.

Today, as in previous generations, God continues to grace men and women with a vision of what an authentic life can truly be. As they respond generously to God's invitation, these Catholic educators make it possible for youth to encounter the Risen Lord, Who teaches the way, the truth, and the life (John 14:6).

Our heritage of faith emphatically proclaims the Good News that it is the Risen Lord Himself teaching and administering through those truly excellent Catholic educators who are ever mindful of their vocation and endeavor to express it through all that they do.

References

Ackerman, R. H., Donaldson, G. A., & van der Bogert, R. (1996). *Making sense as a school leader: Persisting questions, creative opportunities.* San Francisco, CA: Jossey-Bass.

Beck, L. G., & Murphy, J. (1992). Searching for a robust understanding of the principalship. *Educational Administration Quarterly, 28*(3), 387-396.

Bryce, M. C. (1978). Four decades of Roman Catholic innovators. *Religious Education, 73*, S36-S57.

Bryk, A. S., Lee, V. E., & Holland, P. B. (1993). *Catholic schools and the common good.* Cambridge, MA: Harvard University Press.

Burlingame, M., & Sergiovanni, T. (1993). Some questions about school leadership and communication theory. *Journal of Management Systems, 5*(2), 51-61.

Callahan, R. E. (1962). *Education and the cult of efficiency: A study of the social forces that have shaped the administration of the public schools.* Chicago: The University of Chicago Press.

Coleman, J. S. (1987a). Families and schools. *Educational Researcher, 6*, 32-38.

Coleman, J. S. (1987b). Social capital and the development of youth. *Momentum, 18*(19), 6-8.

Coleman, J. S. (1991). *Parental involvement in education.* Washington, DC: U.S. Department of Education.

Coleman, J., Hoffer, T., & Kilgore, S. (1982). *High school achievement: Public, Catholic and private schools compared.* New York: Basic Books.

Coleman, J., & Hoffer, T. (1987). *Public and private high schools: The impact of communities.* New York: Basic Books.

Convey, J. (1992). *Catholic schools make a difference: Twenty-five years of research.* Washington, DC: National Catholic Educational Association.

Dewey, J. (1916, 1944). *Democracy and education: An introduction to the philosophy of education.* New York: Free Press.

Dulles, A. (1988). *The reshaping of Catholicism: Current challenges in the theology of church.* New York: Harper & Row.

Foster, W. P. (1980a). The changing administrator: Developing managerial praxis. *Eductional Theory, 30*(1), 11-23.

Foster, W. P. (1980b). Administration and the crisis in legitimacy: A review of Habermasian thought. *Harvard Educational Review, 50*(4), 496-505.

Frase, L., & Hetzel, R. (1990). *School management by wandering around.* Lancaster, PA: Technomic Publishing Company, Inc.

Getzels, J. W., & Guba, E. G. (1957). Social behavior and the administrative process. *The School Review, 29*, 30-40.

Griffiths, D. E. (1988). Administrative theory. In N. Boyan (Ed.), *Handbook of research on educational administration* (pp. 27-51). New York: Longman.

Herzberg, F. (1966). *Work and the nature of man.* New York: World Publishing.

Hirsch, E. J. (1987). *Cultural literacy: What every American needs to know.* Boston: Houghton Mifflin Company.

Jacobs, R. M. (1995). *The grammar of Catholic schooling: Implications for Catholic educational leaders.* Washington, DC: United States Catholic Conference.

John Paul II. (1987). Address to teachers. *Origins, 17*(17), 279-281.

John Paul II. (1995). *The gospel of life: Evangelium vitae.* Boston, MA: Pauline Books and Media.

Kagan, D. M. (1992). Professional growth among preservice and beginning teachers. *Review of Educational Research, 62*(2), 129-169.

Lannie, V. P., & Diethorn, B. C. (1968, Spring). For the honor and glory of God: The Philadelphia bible riots of 1840. *History of Education Quarterly, 8*, 44-106.

Leo XIII. (1887, 1979). Common duties and interests. In The Benedictine Monks of Solesemes, *Education: Papal teachings* (A. Robeschini, Trans., pp. 104-108). Boston: St. Paul Editions.

Leo XIII. (1888, 1979). Freedom of education. In The Benedictine Monks of Solesemes, *Education: Papal teachings* (A. Robeschini, Trans., pp. 110-115). Boston: St. Paul Editions.

Leo XIII. (1897, 1979). Education at the service of faith. In The Benedictine Monks of Solesemes, *Education: Papal teachings* (A. Robeschini, Trans., pp. 129-35). Boston: St. Paul Editions.

Maritain, J. (1943). *Education at the crossroads.* New Haven, CN: Yale University Press.

Mazlow, A. (1943). A theory of human motivation. *Psychological Review, 50*(2), 370-396.

McCadden, J. J. (1964-1965). Bishop Hughes versus the Public School Scoiety of New York. *Catholic Historical Review, 50*, 188-207.

Medved, M. (1996). *Saving childhood: How to protect your children.* New York: Harper-Collins.

Meyers, B. (1941) *The education of sisters: A plan for integrating the religious, social, cultural and professional training of teachers.* New York: Sheed and Ward.

Murphy, J. (1992). *The landscape of leadership preparation: Reframing the education of school administrators.* Newbury Park, CA: Corwin Press, Inc.

Murphy, J. (1993). Alternative designs, new directions. In J. Murphy (Ed.), *Preparing tomorrow's school leaders: Alternative designs.* University Park, PA: UCEA.

Murphy, J. F. (1973, Spring). The contribution of the human sciences to the pedagogy of Thomas E. Shields. *The Living Light, 10,* 79-87.

Murphy, J. F. (1974, Winter). Thomas Edward Shields: Progressive religious educator. *Notre Dame Journal of Education, 5,* 4, 358-368.

National Conference of Catholic Bishops. (1972, 1984). To teach as Jesus did, a pastoral message on Catholic education. In H. J. Nolan (Ed.), *Pastoral letters of the United States Catholic Bishops (Vol. 3,* pp. 306-340). Washington, DC: National Catholic Conference of Bishops/ United States Catholic Conference.

Newman, J. H. (1927, 1987). *The idea of a university defined and illustrated.* Chicago: Loyola University Press.

Pelikan, J. (1985). The rabbi. In *Jesus through the centuries* (pp. 9-20). New Haven, CN: Yale University Press.

Pius IX. (1864, 1979). Secularism in education. In The Benedictine Monks of Solesemes, *Education: Papal teachings* (A. Robeschini, Trans., pp. 49-53). Boston: St. Paul Editions.

Pius IX. (1875, 1979). Attendance at non-Catholic schools. In The Benedictine Monks of Solesemes, *Education: Papal teachings* (A. Robeschini, Trans., pp. 66-70). Boston: St. Paul Editions.

Pius X. (1905, 1946). *On the teaching of Christian doctrine.* Boston: Daughters of St. Paul.

Pius XI. (1929). *The Christian education of youth.* Boston: Daughters of St. Paul.

Pius XII. (1945, 1979). The vocation of the teacher. In The Benedictine Monks of Solesemes, *Education: Papal teachings* (A. Robeschini, Trans., pp. 336-345). Boston: St. Paul Editions.

Pius XII. (1954a, 1979). The condition of the Christian teacher. In The Benedictine Monks of Solesemes, *Education: Papal teachings* (A. Robeschini, Trans., pp. 476-481). Boston: St. Paul Editions.

Pius XII. (1954b, 1979). Good teachers. In The Benedictine Monks of Solesemes, *Education: Papal teachings* (A. Robeschini, Trans., pp. 482-485). Boston: St. Paul Editions.

Pius XII. (1955, 1979). Redemption and education. In The Benedictine Monks of Solesemes, *Education: Papal teachings* (A. Robeschini, Trans., pp. 500-503). Boston: St. Paul Editions.

Pius XII. (1958, 1979). The Catholic school in the face of the realities of the modern world. In The Benedictine Monks of Solesemes, *Education: Papal teachings* (A. Robeschini, Trans., pp. 573-578). Boston: St. Paul Editions.

Prestine, N. A., & Thurston, P. W. (Eds.). (1994). New directions in educational administration: Policy, preparation, and practice. *Advances in educational administration* (Volume 3). Greenwich, CN: JAI Press Inc.

Ryan, F. J. (1991, Spring). Monsignor John Bonner and progressive education in the Archdiocese of Philadelphia, 1925-1945. *Records of the American Catholic Historical Society of Philadelphia, 102*(1-2), 17-43.

Sacred Congregation for Catholic Education. (1977, 1982). Catholic schools. In A. Flannery (Ed.), *Vatican Council II the conciliar and post-conciliar documents* (Vol. 2, rev. ed., pp. 602-29). Northport, NY: Costello Publishing Co.

Sacred Congregation for Catholic Education. (1982). Lay Catholics in schools: Witnesses to the faith. In A. Flannery (Ed.), *Vatican Council II the conciliar and post-conciliar documents* (Vol. 2, rev. ed., pp. 630-661). Northport, NY: Costello Publishing Co.

Senge, P. M. (1990). *The fifth discipline: The art & practice of the learning organization.* New York: Doubleday.

Sergiovanni, T. J. (1994). *Building community in schools.* San Francisco: Jossey-Bass.

Sergiovanni, T. J. (1995). *The principalship: A reflective-practice perspective* (3rd ed.). Needham Heights, MA: Allyn and Bacon.

Shields, T. E. (1907). *The education of our girls.* New York: Benzinger Brothers.

Shields, T. E. (1919). The need of the Catholic Sisters College and the scope of its work. *The Catholic Educational Review, XVII*, 6, 420.

Silberman, C. (1970). *Crisis in the classroom.* New York: Random House.

Smylie, M. A. Teacher participation in school decision making: Assessing willingness to participate. *Educational Evaluation and Policy Analysis, 14*(1), 53-67.

Starratt, R. J. (1994). *Building an ethical school: A practical response to the moral crisis in schools.* Bristol, PA: The Falmer Press.

Tyack, D. & Hansot, E. (1982). *Managers of virtue: Public school leadership in America, 1820-1980.* New York: Basic Books.

United States Catholic Conference. (1993, 1994). *Formation and development for Catholic school leaders* (Maria J. Ciriello, OP, Ed.). Washington, DC: United States Catholic Conference.

Vaill, P. B. (1986). The purposing of high-performing systems. In T. J. Sergiovanni & J. E. Corbally (Eds.), *Leadership and organizational culture* (pp. 89-104). Urbana, IL: University of Illinois Press.

Vatican Council II. (1965a, 1988). Declaration on Christian education. In A. Flannery (Ed.), *Vatican Council II the conciliar and post-conciliar documents* (Vol. 1, rev. ed., pp. 725-737). Northport, NY: Costello Publishing Co.

Vatican Council II. (1965b, 1988). Decree on the apostolate of lay people. In A. Flannery (Ed.), *Vatican Council II the conciliar and post-conciliar documents* (Vol. 1, rev. ed., pp. 766-798). Northport, NY: Costello Publishing Co.

Vatican Council II. (1965c, 1988). Pastoral constitution on the Church in the modern world. In A. Flannery (Ed.), *Vatican Council II the conciliar and post-conciliar documents* (Vol. 1, rev. ed., pp. 903-1014). Northport, NY: Costello Publishing Co.

Weick, K. E. (1984). Small wins: Redefining the scale of social problems. *American Psychologist, 39*(1), 40-49.

Willms, J. D. (1984). School effectiveness within the public and private sectors: An evaluation. *Evaluation Review, 8*, 113-135.

Willms, J. D. (1985). Catholic-school effects on academic achievement: New evidence from the High School and Beyond Follow-Up Study. *Sociology of Education, 58*, 98-114.

Willms, J. D. (1987). Patterns of academic achievement in public and private schools: Implications for public policy and future research. In E. H. Haertel, T. James & H. M. Levin (Eds.), *Comparing public & private schools* (Vol. 2: School achievement). New York: Falmer Press.

Ward, J. (1947). *Thomas Edward Shields: Biologist, psychologist, educator.* New York: Scribner's Sons.

Wohlwent, M. V. (1968). *The educational principles of Dr. Thomas E. Shields and their impact on his teacher training program at the Catholic University of America.* Unpublished doctoral dissertation, Catholic University of America.

Notes